SHAKESPEARE
and the
Birmingham
Repertory Theatre
1913–1929

Claire Cochrane

THE SOCIETY FOR THEATRE RESEARCH

First published in 1993
by The Society for Theatre Research
c/o The Theatre Museum, 1E Tavistock Street
Covent Garden, London WC2E 7PA

ISBN 0 85430 053 8

This book is dedicated to my mother Nora Davies
who first took me to Birmingham Rep
and to my husband John Cochrane
who has shared and maintained my theatregoing habit

Typeset by EMS Photosetters, Thorpe Bay, Essex
Printed by Woolnough Bookbinding
of Irthlingborough, Northants.

Contents

Acknowledgements

I would like to thank Jennifer Aylmer, Janet Birkett, Nancy Burman, Jean Campbell, Sonia Drake, Tom English, Robert Evans, John Greenwood, Finlay James, Joe Mitchenson, Tessa Sidey, I. A. Shapiro, Graham Winteringham, Physhe Wright, Niky Rathbone, Steve Haste and the staff of the Language and Literature Department of Birmingham Central Library, the staff of the Birmingham Repertory Theatre, the staff of the Theatre Museum and the Shakespeare Centre, Stratford-upon-Avon. Jim Davies and Paul Cooper copied photographs for me. I am also grateful that I was able to talk to the late Dame Gwen Frangçon-Davies and J. C. Trewin. I owe special thanks to the staff of the Shakespeare Institute but in particular Susan Brock for her painstaking assistance, and Russell Jackson who initiated my research on the Rep, supervised my thesis and finally helped to edit the book for publication.

All photographs are reproduced by permission of the Sir Barry Jackson Trust.

List of Illustrations

Frontispiece: Barry Jackson as Feste, 1904

Between pages 70-71

1. *Measure for Measure* – The Pilgrim Players (1910)
2. *King John* – The Pilgrim Players (1911)
3. Ivor Barnard as Shylock (1913 and 1915)
4. Margaret Chatwin as Beatrice (1919 and 1920)
5. Set for *Love's Labour's Lost* (1919 and 1920)
6. Set for *Much Ado About Nothing* (1919 and 1920)
7. *Henry IV Part One* (1920 and 1921)
8. Set for Senate scene, *Othello* (1920)
9. Set for *Romeo and Juliet* (1922)

Between pages 96-97

10. *Romeo and Juliet* (1922)
11. E Stuart Vinden as Rumour in *Henry IV Part Two* (1921)
12. E Stuart Vinden as Othello (1920)
13. *Romeo and Juliet* (Regent Theatre, 1924)
14. *Hamlet* (Kingsway Theatre, 1925)
15. *All's Well That Ends Well* (1927)
16. *Macbeth* (Royal Court Theatre, 1928)
17. *The Taming of the Shrew* (Royal Court Theatre, 1928)
18. A company read-through in the Rep foyer (1926)

Barry Jackson as Feste, 1904

'Mr Barry Jackson: runs repertory at Birmingham;
repertory is out of date; and where on earth is Birmingham?'

Harley Granville Barker, letter to Phyllis Whitworth, 11 February 1924

Introduction

Between 1913, when the Birmingham Repertory Theatre opened, and 1971 when the company moved into a new building, no other British theatre apart from the Old Vic and the Shakespeare Memorial Theatre staged more productions of Shakespeare. Indeed when J. L. Styan described in his book *The Shakespeare Revolution* the transformation in Shakespeare production values which has taken place in the twentieth century, he emphasised the contribution of the Rep and its founder Sir Barry Jackson.[1] Jackson's life and the work of the theatre he built span almost exactly the period covered by Styan's book. Styan begins with the Victorian actor-managers who first stimulated Jackson's love of Shakespeare and then provoked him into joining the rebellion against their dominance. When the old Rep closed in 1971, Peter Brook's production of *A Midsummer Night's Dream* — the production which Styan considers ended 'the first phase of the story'[2] of the Shakespeare revolution, was still in the repertoire of the Royal Shakespeare Company. Brook directed his first professional production of Shakespeare (*King John*) at the Rep in 1945. The following year Jackson, as Director of the Stratford Festival, invited Brook to stage what became a landmark production of *Love's Labour's Lost* at the Shakespeare Memorial Theatre. And so Brook became part of the Rep legend — a legend which embraced other leading figures in British theatre history: Laurence Olivier, Ralph Richardson, John Gielgud, Gwen Frangçon-Davies, Peggy Ashcroft and Edith Evans and later Paul Scofield, Margaret Leighton, Albert Finney and Derek Jacobi. All owed early acting opportunities to Barry Jackson's company.

This book began life as a doctoral thesis on the history of Rep

1

Shakespeare until 1971. It was an attempt to establish the factual basis for the legend and place the achievement of one provincial theatre company firmly within the context of the twentieth-century stage production of Shakespeare as a whole. The final result was not an account of a succession of major productions and great performances — the staple ingredients of traditional theatre history. The Birmingham Repertory Theatre bred great actors, but this was a by-product of Jackson's policies, which nourished youthful innovation rather than assured excellence. The Birmingham productions rarely ran for more than a few weeks (in the early years there was a weekly change of play) and performance standards varied considerably — the consequence of the strains of the short-run repertory system. Although there were important productions, the Rep's contribution to British theatre was the cumulative effect of sixty years of consistent experiment and practice.

That said, this book begins with the production of *Twelfth Night* which opened the Rep in 1913, and then effectively ends with the modern-dress productions which were staged in Birmingham and London during the 1920s. This has enabled me to explore very fully Jackson's personal commitment to Shakespeare, his Birmingham context and the background to the establishment first of the Pilgrim Players (Jackson's early amateur group), and then the opening of the Rep itself — the first purpose-built British repertory theatre. I have also explained why the simultaneous introduction of a new system of theatrical organisation and a new approach to the production of Shakespeare at the beginning of this century was part of a major cultural shift. The history of Shakespeare on the stage reflects the overall history of European theatre. Each change of direction and each new theatrical aesthetic seems to be matched by a corresponding need to go on performing Shakespeare. Barry Jackson was by education and inclination a European who had a considerable knowledge of the theory and practice of theatrical innovation which began to sweep across Europe towards Great Britain at the end of the nineteenth century. The third chapter of this book analyses the wide range of influences which led to Jackson's first amateur experiments with Shakespeare and formed the foundation for the Rep's staging methods. The Pilgrim productions, as well as the work during the theatre's first decade which is discussed in the fourth chapter, reveal both the extent of Jackson's practical involvement with the theatre he created and the contribution of friends and colleagues such as John Drinkwater and Bache Matthews, the actors who made up the company, directorial and textual policies and the approach to design.

As an actor and director, Jackson was by no means as gifted as his contemporary Harley Granville Barker. Jackson was, however, a designer of considerable taste and originality. In 1934, Cecil Chisholm remarked that he 'was a model for most designers in one rare quality — his capacity to design in only three or four colours . . . he was one of the first English designers to work in the round'[3]. John Drinkwater wrote: 'I always felt that as a producer too much of his attention was given to the decorative aspects of his play at the expense of the acting . . . with the exception of Claude Lovat Fraser I have known no stage designer . . . with so sure an eye for the general effect of a scene, or with so certain a sense of the practical possibilities of material'[4].

By 1919, when the company first mounted a production in London (John Drinkwater's *Abraham Lincoln*), the theatre was beginning to attract professional artists of very high calibre. The fifth chapter focuses on the effect of directors such as A. E. Filmer and H. K. Ayliff and the arrival of Paul Shelving who remained the Rep's principal designer until Jackson's death in 1961. The chapter culminates in an account of Ayliff's 1922 production of *Romeo and Juliet* which in 1924, with John Gielgud as Romeo and Gwen Frangçon-Davies as Juliet, became the first Rep Shakespeare to be seen in London. The sixth and seventh chapters concentrate on the six modern-dress productions staged between 1923 and 1929. By then it should be clear how much these major ventures owed to the consistent policies of earlier years. However the importance of the modern-dress experiments cannot be over-emphasised. They provoked a radical psychological change in twentieth-century attitudes towards Shakespeare which is still felt in present-day production.

1929 marked an hiatus in Rep Shakespeare which lasted for several years and thus seemed an appropriate point to stop detailed analysis. As I explain in a brief epilogue, Jackson and his colleagues continued to have an impact on Shakespeare production, especially during Jackson's tenure at the Shakespeare Memorial Theatre between 1946 and 1948. Also the Birmingham productions of the three *Henry VI* plays, finally staged as a complete trilogy in 1953 in Birmingham and London, were responsible for the theatrical and scholarly rehabilitation of hitherto neglected works. But the essential groundwork in Shakespeare innovation was achieved by the end of the 1920s. What happened later simply carried on the same firmly-held ideology which gave members of the company the freedom and security to develop the talent and creativity which reached out from a small, unpretentious building in Birmingham to benefit the entire British theatre.

Chapter One
The First Night

The Birmingham Repertory Theatre opened on Saturday 13 February 1913 with a production of *Twelfth Night*. It is ironic that the theatre which was to launch the careers of some of the greatest twentieth-century Shakespearian actors inaugurated its existence with a production where there was nothing remarkable about individual performances. Indeed several, betraying no doubt their amateur origins, were little more than competent. One 'John Darnley' bewildered some observers by playing Malvolio as a 'skittish French fop' rather than 'the "kind of Puritan" that Andrew hated'. He was 'either a young man trying to be old or an old man trying to be young'. The critic of the *Daily Telegraph* suggested that his performance was rather in the tradition of Beerbohm Tree's 'fantastical conception' than Henry Ainley's more austere approach in Harley Granville Barker's recent production at the Savoy Theatre in London. A few months after the Birmingham first night it would be possible to see Tree's Malvolio (followed astonishingly by four minor Malvolios) during the ninth annual Shakespeare Festival mounted at His Majesty's Theatre in London. Also that summer, in Stratford-upon-Avon, Frank Benson would play the abused steward yet again to a faithful audience who may well have seen substantially the same performance (not his best) many times since he first staged his production in 1892. Whatever their faults and idiosyncracies, however, there could be no doubt that Tree in London and Benson in the provinces were stars with enormous personal followings: no human stars appeared in the Birmingham firmament that mild February night.

The star of the evening was in fact the theatre itself: the first

5

purpose-built repertory theatre in Great Britain. The enthusiastic audience was packed into an auditorium from which all the traditional embellishments had been banished. There were 'no red plush tip-up chairs to tire the eye, no splenetic goddesses in plaster frowning over the stage, no gaudy gilts and golds, no urgent pleas for whisky, tobacco or soap, shrieked from a publicity-pimpled screen' (*Westminster Gazette*).[1] Everything was in exquisite taste. Sir Oliver Lodge, the Principal of Birmingham University, who read the first night telegrams from the stage, called it 'a beautiful brown building'. The prevailing colour was brown: the velvet drop curtain, the leather seats, the dark oak walls with panels of gold canvas and the oak round the gallery and over the proscenium frame which was inlaid with ebony and satin wood. The vestibule entrance and staircase were in white Sicilian and brown Napoleon marble. The walls of the lounge at the back of the theatre were covered with brown paper and there was a marble floor. The most striking feature of the auditorium was its size and shape: the total seating capacity was 464 with 200 accommodated in the balcony.

The other principal playhouses in Birmingham were much bigger. The rebuilt Theatre Royal, decorated in green, white and gold, had opened in 1904 with seating for 2,200 and the Grand, Prince of Wales, Alexandra and Hippodrome theatres were of similar size. The three opulent blue and gold horse-shoe balconies of the Prince of Wales theatre were typical of late Victorian theatrical emphasis on social interaction and ostentatious display by the management and among the audience. At the Rep the steep straight rake of the seating, with no divisions apart from the balcony, was designed to focus attention on the play itself. Every patron had a clear view of the stage as the dramatic critic of the *Liverpool Courier* explained: 'Right from immediately in front of the stage rises row behind row of seats practically in straight lines, each behind the first set so toweringly high above the row in front that the most upsoaring headgear need have no terrors for a playgoer of diminutive size'. The plans for the step-floor had to overcome opposition from the local magistrates, who originally voted it as dangerous. Even today, eighty years on, the steepness of the rake comes as a shock.

The stage was small: 42 feet deep and 28 feet wide (the stage of the Theatre Royal was 46 feet deep but 72 feet at its widest). The usual orchestra pit was missing. Instead there was an apron stage with a removable floor, so that a small orchestra could play if required. Doors on either side of the proscenium opened on to the apron and were used in performance. The pale blue 'heaven' attracted a good deal of interest. In place of the traditional flat back-cloth depicting outdoor scenes, there was a large elliptical plaster cyclorama fixed permanently about $2\frac{1}{2}$ feet from the back wall of the stage and extending some forty feet up. Several reviews commented on the beautiful effect of limitless sky achieved for Olivia's garden as two strong lights were shone on to the cyclorama from the back of the auditorium. There were no footlights but two limelights positioned on perch platforms were mounted in the wings. The Fortuny lighting system which reflected light through bands of coloured silk was not installed in time for the first night but the special opportunities to achieve a subtle range of light and colour afforded by this new apparatus were eagerly anticipated. Certainly there were a few technical hitches at the first performance, when legs were illuminated rather than faces. What must have been obvious to all, however, was that there was no question of mounting the kind of massively sumptuous stage settings for Shakespeare which Tree had made so popular in London or which were displayed by provincial imitators like Richard Flanagan in Manchester. Touring versions of the excesses of both could be seen in Birmingham at the Theatre Royal or the Prince of Wales. At the Rep there was simply no room. The new playhouse was built to sustain a radically new theatrical aesthetic.

As director of *Twelfth Night* Barry Jackson staged the play virtually uncut, within three hours and with just one fifteen minute interval. As designer, he was content to achieve colour and suggestion without recourse to the sort of elaborate scenic realism which in traditional productions meant substantial textual losses, transposition of scenes and lengthy waits for set changes. The swiftness of action was achieved by using the minimum of stage furniture and the use of a temporary inner proscenium combined with curtains to create three distinct acting areas. The interiors of both Orsino's palace and Olivia's house were suggested by different canvas back-cloths placed some five feet up on the main stage and painted to represent antique tapestries. Plain canvas-covered rectangular frames served for seats. The proscenium doors were used as entrances on to the apron for Viola's arrival in Illyria and short linking 'street' scenes which were played in front of a plain blue curtain. A set model photographed for a later exhibition shows the design for an exterior scene which consisted of a group of pillars placed stage left on the central acting area, with two wide concave steps leading to a raised inner stage at the back where one formal tree shape can be seen. In performance the 'garden scenes' apparently looked very beautiful, with a simple balustrade positioned in front of the blue cyclorama.

The costuming would seem to have been resolutely traditional: that is Elizabethan but with Victorian modifications. Viola wore the conventional quasi-Greek, supposedly Illyrian national dress with a full-skirted short robe, sash and cap, while Feste sported an extravagantly horned jester's cap. In 1934 Cecil Chisholm remembered that Olivia's household were dressed all in black.[2] Some first-night reviews objected to the 'weeping raiment' (which is now customary in costume designs for the play), but the *Westminster Gazette* pointed out that Olivia is said to have been 'watering each day her chamber round with tears for her dead brother'. Felix Aylmer, who played Orsino, had come straight from a small role in the Savoy production in which he had also understudied Orsino. He later recalled that so accustomed had he been to Granville Barker's less traditional costuming that at the Rep, in a fit of nerves, he forgot to put on his short puffed breeches and played the first scene with only his tights under his doublet.[3]

The uneven standard of acting clearly reflected the widely differing backgrounds of the cast. Aylmer's apprenticeship had included work with Tree and Fred Terry as well as Granville Barker, but now his performance was undistinguished. He could not make much impression as Orsino — a character scorned by the critic of the *Birmingham Daily Post*. 'He is a sentimentalist without virility .. Mr Felix Aylmer, cast for such a role, could only do his best, and that, to give him his due, he did'. W. Ripton Haines, an ex-Bensonian, however, earned praise for presenting Sir Toby not as the usual drunken buffoon, but as a gentleman, especially in his fight with Sebastian. Scott Sunderland, another Bensonian, was hailed by the *Liverpool Courier* as one of the unequivocal successes of the evening, playing a 'buoyant, tuneful and sweet voiced' Feste. E. A. Baughan, writing in the *Daily News and Leader*, felt that he 'properly suggested some of the romance and pathos of the chorus of the play'. The three principal women's roles were taken by former members of Jackson's amateur company, the Pilgrim Players. Margaret Chatwin as Olivia was little more than dignified while Cathleen Orford as Maria was variously described as 'sprightly' or 'mischievous'. Jackson's niece Cecily Byrne, who played Viola, provoked a mixed response. The critic of the *Westminster Gazette*, recalling past performances which had turned Viola into another Rosalind, liked Cecily Byrne's 'tremulous charm and wistful grace' which he felt were true to the text. Other commentators felt that she lacked emotional depth and was inadequate for the lyrical demands of the part. In general the man from the *Liverpool Courier* was not inclined to be sympathetic. He acknowledged the value of simplicity and suggestiveness in staging but with reservations: 'the over-elaboration and costliness of stage production need to be opposed, but if too many aids to illusion on the stage are dispensed with, acting of a supremely excellent order must be requisitioned to supply the deficiency.'

Barry Jackson and his company might well have replied that supremely excellent acting was not their prime concern. The *Birmingham Gazette* summed up what appeared to be the most important factor in the enterprise: 'What a joy to abolish the picture-show Shakespeare with the little constellation revolving feebly around some glorious sun! In these days to have a play cast evenly and with due regard for those all important persons, the minor characters, is an event for which we cannot be sufficiently thankful.' Despite the problematic performances, the occasional technical gaffe and perhaps most significantly the disconcerting clash at moments between tradition and innovation, seasoned theatrical observers would have been aware that this event stood at the interface between opposing factions in the British theatre as a whole and in the production of Shakespeare in particular. In London the previous autumn, Harley Granville Barker's productions of *The Winter's Tale* and *Twelfth Night* had effectively polarised audience opinion, defiantly combining the scenic values of the new stagecraft with ensemble acting of the highest quality. Less glamorously, in December 1912 at the King's Hall in Covent Garden, the implacable

Elizabethanist William Poel staged *Troilus and Cressida*, a play virtually unheard of outside the Shakespeare reading societies, with the unknown Edith Evans as Cressida.

Reviewers of the Birmingham *Twelfth Night* were quick to nail their colours to the mast and several compared it with the Savoy productions. Norman Wilkinson's dazzling white set and apron stage built for *The Winter's Tale* over the Savoy orchestra pit had aroused controversy. E. A. Baughan remarked that he preferred the subtler effect of the Rep's cyclorama and smaller, higher brown apron stage. The clear division between the Rep's forestage and the front row of auditorium seating was probably less threatening to audiences unused to close contact with actors in performance. The critic of the *Birmingham Mail* worried a little about Jackson's plain blue traverse curtains. Wilkinson had used decorative curtains which indicated location. Jackson's curtains, Baughan felt, 'carried simplification a long way for an ordinary audience'. For the *Standard* critic on the other hand, the unlocalised setting allowed full concentration on the play. The nature of stage illusion itself was central to the debate. The *Liverpool Courier* declared that the new method had little advantage over the traditional drop scenes which were painted to represent actual locations. He specifically objected that the scene where Malvolio reads Maria's letter 'lost much of its savour' because Sir Toby, Sir Andrew and Fabian were positioned on the apron 'and consequently had no appearance of being in the same scene as Malvolio himself'. He continued, 'If the ideal of the new method be to afford stimulus to the imagination, to be prodigal of firm suggestiveness instead of apparent realism, it seems antagonistic to the ideal to make the scene needlessly difficult of visualisation'. Baughan decided that Jackson had obviously copied the scenic elements of Barker's productions and added the warning: 'It is to be hoped that the Savoy productions are not to establish a convention which will be just as bad as the convention of realistic scenery.' Had Baughan been present at the previous productions of Shakespeare by the Pilgrim Players he might have reconsidered his opinion that Jackson had simply copied Barker. In any case, as time would show, the new convention was here to stay.

Before the performance began, Barry Jackson read a celebratory ode by John Drinkwater, the theatre's General Manager. Acting under the name of John Darnley, Drinkwater also played Malvolio. Drinkwater, already a published poet and soon to be acknowledged formally along with others such as Rupert Brooke and John Masefield as one of the Georgian poets who aimed to regenerate the moribund condition of English verse, here wrote with an impassioned rhetoric which today seems embarrassingly portentous. Typically the man from the *Liverpool Courier* found the proclaimed ideals a little too rich to stomach. Drinkwater listed the great dramatists of the past ranging from the Greeks through Shakespeare to the eighteenth century, concluding with the more literary of modern dramatists: Galsworthy, Barker and Yeats. The critic took exception to what came next, thinking Drinkwater 'churlish perhaps, in his implications as to the unworthiness of the ordinary stage efforts':

> In these walls
> Look not for that light trickery that falls
> To death at birth, wrought piecemeal at the will
> Of Apes who seek to ply their mimic skill:
> Here shall the player work as work he may,
> Yet shall he work in service of the play.

The Liverpudlian observer responded rather sourly to what he called 'the orthodox Repertory faith' and continued:

> Indeed the whole of Mr Drinkwater's ode set one furiously thinking, wondering whether the devotees of the Repertory movement know anything of English dramatic history prior to the rise of Mr Granville Barker; ever heard of a Bancroft management, of a Lyceum that once was; of the rich variety of Tree's manifold effects; of the magnificent services to modern drama rendered by Sir George Alexander; of dramatists named Barrie and Pinero; and wondering too, whether these same perfervid devotees are not more enthralled by mere names than ever was the most commercial and commonplace of actor-managers.

By 1913 it was hardly surprising that proponents of the repertory movement should consider it necessary to adopt an aggressively embattled stance. The struggle had been going on for a long time. Since 1879, the year of Barry Jackson's birth, when Matthew Arnold published his essay 'The French Play in London' advocating the establishment of a state-subsidised National Theatre and a network of provincial municipal theatres, would-be reformers like William Archer and George Bernard Shaw had fulminated against the glossy, star-dominated triviality of late Victorian theatre. Thoughtful new drama which dealt with serious issues was either too gloomy or too frank to achieve acceptance. Aspiring actors were sacrificed to the egos of the actor–managers and the once-flourishing provincial stock companies were swept away as stars like Henry Irving and Ellen Terry, benefiting from cheap rail travel and popular press publicity, were able to tour complete London productions. As the new century dawned, however, the ruinous expense of what Drinkwater later dubbed the 'one man show',[4] combined with the enormous ground rents of London theatres and the increased tendency for family systems of theatrical management to be taken over by impersonal financial syndicates, were gradually destroying the actor–manager system. Young actors were chained to minor roles in long runs of commercially popular plays maintained by businessmen more interested in profit than artistic management. The memoirs of Basil Dean and Ben Iden Payne, both future leaders of the new movement, bear ample witness to the exhaustion and insecurity of the life of the touring actor forced to travel round the country with battered mechanical copies of London successes.[5] The repertory ideal looked forward to the possibility of theatres where well-balanced companies of players, freed from commercial pressures by some miracle of public or private patronage, could perform a wide variety of modern and classic plays in rapid succession.

In order to make the dream a reality, however, it was necessary to overcome both the problem of finance and the innate conservatism of British audiences. 'Art has no possible relation to money' wrote Barry Jackson in 1924 (ironically after dwindling audiences had forced him to close the theatre), 'the spiritual cannot be estimated by the material'.[6] But these were the words of a rich man. Jackson's inherited wealth derived from the hard-nosed business acumen of his father, the Victorian provision merchant George Jackson. George Jackson's Maypole Dairy Company financed a family environment devoted to the love of literature, art and above all

12

theatre. During Barry Jackson's childhood theatre had become increasingly middle-class and respectable. The cultural revival of the late nineteenth century — the efforts to bring about social reform, universal suffrage and wider educational opportunity — owed much to Britain's industrial and commercial wealth. The high priest of Victorian aesthetic values, John Ruskin, owed his fortune to the family trade in fine sherry and the Shakespeare Memorial Theatre was built with the wealth earned from Flower's beer. The first regional repertory theatres were nourished by the grocer's shop. Annie Horniman, who financed the opening of the Abbey Theatre in Dublin in 1904 and the first English repertory company at the Gaiety theatre in Manchester in 1908, was rich because of the popularity of the packeted tea which bore her family's name. The Glasgow and Liverpool ventures, though neither owed their support to single wealthy patrons, were launched in 1909 and 1911 with backing from leading figures in industry and commerce conscious of the need to improve the cultural credentials of their fast-growing cities. As in London where the 1904–7 repertory experiments by Granville Barker and J. E. Vedrenne at the Court Theatre produced ensemble acting of the highest quality and finally established Shaw as a dramatist of major importance, the benefits of the new system for major theatrical reform were obvious. The plays of serious dramatists like J. M. Synge, John Galsworthy, John Masefield and Stanley Houghton were staged professionally for the first time as well as the work of European dramatists like Chekhov and Gorky. A new generation of actors such as Madge Mackintosh, Harcourt Williams, Lewis Casson and Sybil Thorndike had become accustomed to working together with a new kind of stage director, frequently not acting himself, who put the overall presentation of the play before the kudos of the principal actor.

Unfortunately in these days before the notion of state and civic subsidy of the arts gained general currency, the difficulties of maintaining financial viability were enormous. 'When is a repertory theatre not a repertory theatre?' Beerbohm Tree is reputed to have quipped. 'When it's a success of course!'[7] In London Barker's long-term aim behind his repertory project, the establishment of a permanent London-based National Theatre, failed, as did Herbert Trench's repertory season at the Haymarket in 1909 and Charles

Frohman's experiment with 'true repertory' at the Duke of York's which Barker largely directed. London audiences found 'true' repertory, a variety of plays acted in nightly succession, difficult to accept. What had proved workable at the small Court Theatre did not succeed at the larger Savoy where Barker and Vedrenne were again in partnership between 1907-8. Barker had to content himself with offering advice and support to the new provincial theatres. These were generally 'short run' theatres where the permanent company performed plays for a fixed period of one to three weeks. Even so there were strains created by the role of the private patron. In Dublin the Irish Players' desire for autonomy, and resentment of a foreigner's charity caused Annie Horniman to transfer her largesse to the new Manchester venture where both her first director Ben Iden Payne and then Lewis Casson had cause to doubt her artistic judgement — doubts which were to be justified in 1917 when the permanent company dissolved following Horniman's disastrous decision to put on 'cheery plays' for the duration of the First World War. In Glasgow, the lack of a permanent home, poor audience attendance and the ill-health of Alfred Wareing, the prime mover behind the project, made the Scottish Playgoers' Company ill-equipped to combat the commercial pressures which led to disbandment in 1914. In Liverpool, the Playhouse was run by a board of 'citizen–governors' and a constant financial struggle inevitably meant a compromise between creative experiment and the demands of the ticket-buying public.[8]

The truth was that audiences loved the glamour of actor–manager's theatre, relished sumptuous sets and derived comfort from endless revivals of old favourites like *Charley's Aunt*, *A Royal Divorce* and *The Only Way*. In November 1913, when the initial euphoria created by the new Birmingham theatre had worn off, Barry Jackson commented in a speech to the Sheffield Playgoers' Society:

> It is a thousand pities that we have no better name than the word 'repertory' for our work. It is anything but alluring to the man in the street: 'repeatory' as I once heard it called is almost more suitable. There is a flavour of Socialism, Suffragettes and advanced thought about it which terrifies politicians and sends cold shudders through frequenters of the music hall.[9]

14

In its early days the Rep made few gestures towards the traditional expectations of commercial theatre. There was no blatant puffing in advance publicity. A gong was sounded before each performance to allow the audience a few moments of preparation, almost as if for a religious ceremony. Latecomers were not admitted — indeed there was a grim satisfaction derived from the fact that the only entrances to the auditorium were beside the front row and at the top of the house, which meant maximum embarrassment for anyone who arrived after the start of the play. All tickets could be booked in advance, which was not the usual practice for the cheapest seats in more traditional theatres. There were no rattling teacups at matinées and no bar. In 1913 the programmes, which now did name actors after years of amateur anonymity, were free and there were no curtain calls. There was no attempt to drag reluctant civic dignitaries to gala functions. The Company adopted what Jackson called 'a spartan attitude saying rather brutally "we give our best, take it or leave it."'.[10] But the Rep survived. As Drinkwater pointed out, 'Under the shelter of Jackson's bank balance, the Birmingham theatre was in a position to be as defiant as it liked'.[11] But there was more to it than that. The company had a homogeneous quality lacked by other companies. It was the product of the organic development of a group of like-minded enthusiasts who had worked together for nearly a decade. There was a single-mindedness which accounts for the evangelical zeal of the early years. And whereas Annie Horniman was an outside patron looking for an object of patronage, with Barry Jackson as a homegrown founder of the Rep, patron, producer, designer and actor came together.

There was another important difference in the Rep's order of priorities. The theatre opened with a production of Shakespeare rather than one of the new plays which earlier companies had seen as their main duty to promote. Jackson loved Shakespeare. He was named after George Jackson's favourite Shakespearian actor, Birmingham-born Barry Sullivan. Indeed only a few months before Barry Jackson's birth, Sullivan played Benedick to Helen Faucit's Beatrice in a production of *Much Ado about Nothing* which inaugurated the newly-built Shakespeare Memorial Theatre. Barry Jackson told his Sheffield audience in 1913:

15

I was born with a sense of the theatre. The three volumes of Shakespeare illustrated by Sir John Gilbert have always been and are still my constant companion — one of my early games was to recite, 'double, double, toil and trouble', round an old armchair —and the first play I ever witnessed was *The Taming of the Shrew*. Pantomimes I saw but they did not count — even in those days.[12]

The Rep staged new or controversial realist drama in the early years: plays by Shaw, Galsworthy, Barker and Ibsen. But a balancing emphasis on recent attempts to revive emotionally-heightened or symbolist poetic drama by Maeterlinck, John Masefield, Lascelles Abercrombie, Gordon Bottomley and Drinkwater himself was underpinned by work on Shakespeare, especially innovation in scenic presentation. Also in 1914 there were visits from the Irish Players with a repertoire of work by Synge, Yeats and Lady Gregory; and Jacques Copeau's Théâtre du Vieux Colombier who performed short plays by Alfred de Musset and Molière. The French company played for just one night (24 March 1914) in Station Street, but Copeau's efforts to move away from realism and to bring scenic simplicity, beauty and poetry to classic drama, especially by Molière and Shakespeare, was very much reflected in Jackson's own ideas. For the 1913 Rep season there were eighteenth-century and medieval drama and productions of four other Shakespearian plays. It is clear that the new company was measuring itself against the whole tradition of European drama. P. P. Howe in one of the earliest book-length assessments of the development of the repertory movement believed that the ideal repertory system would eventually break down the barriers between the theatrical and literary worlds.[13] In 1913 in his Sheffield speech, Jackson rejected the notion that the primary objective of a repertory theatre was to produce new plays: 'A repertory theatre should be the home of great masterpieces'. He was not much interested in what he later derided as 'microscopic themes — peering into the back parlours of Manchester'.[14]

However, in order to understand more fully why Jackson and his friends decided to align themselves with the movement to revolutionise the production of Shakespeare, it is necessary to know more about Jackson's background; the reasons why the city of Birmingham proved to be a fertile breeding ground for Shakespearian experiment, and the process which transformed the amateur Pilgrim Players into a professional company.

Chapter Two
Shakespeare, Birmingham and the
Pilgrim Players

The rapidly expanding town of Birmingham where Barry Jackson grew up was peculiarly representative of the extraordinary status of Shakespeare in late Victorian Britain. Across the nation, it was possible to make a living simply reciting Shakespeare. Indeed it has been suggested that William Poel may have first noted the power of simplified staging of Shakespeare by witnessing solo performances of complete plays.[1] As a child Harley Granville Barker, born two years before Barry Jackson in 1877, was put to work with his mother as they toured the country reciting popular poems and extracts from Shakespeare. In Birmingham for much of the second half of the century, enthusiastic audiences from all levels of society enjoyed Shakespeare as much as pantomime and melodrama. Barry Sullivan, George Jackson's favourite, regularly gave his Hamlet, Macbeth or Richard III to packed and noisy houses at the Theatre Royal in the 1870s.[2]

With the proliferation of Shakespeare reading societies and the use of the plays as examination fodder in the developing educational system, Shakespeare had virtually become a national patron saint. In 1874 when F. J. Furnivall founded the New Shakspere Society he declared, 'We cannot have too much of Shakspere. The more we have of the study of him . . . the better we shall be, and the better England will be'.[3] The sentimental patriotism, however, was accompanied by an emphasis on the serious study of Shakespearian texts and Elizabethan staging methods. William Poel's obscure but nonetheless historic 1881 production of the first Quarto of *Hamlet* was inspired by William Grigg's facsimile edition of the first and second Quartos of the play, published in 1880 with an introduction by Furnivall. Poel's production, supported by Furnivall, set in motion a train of scholarly and theatrical endeavour which would ultimately revolutionise Shakespeare in performance.

In Birmingham a declared devotion to Shakespeare was clearly part of the intense social and cultural activity which led to the booming industrial town becoming a city in 1889. "Our Shakespeare Club" was founded in 1862 as primarily a social club for the leading men of the town but one of its aims was the foundation and endowment in 1868 of the Shakespeare Library as part of the newly established Central Reference Library. When the library was badly damaged by fire in 1879 and all but 500 of over 7000 books in the collection were destroyed, public subscription ensured that a new building opened in 1882. By 1903 the printed catalogue listed 11,489 books including a copy of each of the four Shakespeare Folios and rare foreign and illustrated editions. In 1866 the Birmingham Shakespeare Reading Society had been inaugurated with the object of: 'the intelligent reading of the works of Shakespeare; for which purpose a play shall be selected by ballot, and cast by the President . . . similar to the method by which plays are cast for the stage . . . at the end of a scene or scenes, the club shall mutuallly criticise the conception, rendering, and pronunciation of the various parts read'.[4] The dinner held annually to celebrate Shakespeare's birthday invariably included a rousing chorus of *Great Warwickshire Will* — it was still part of the programme in 1902 — as well as the performance of scenes from selected plays. The gravedigger's scene from *Hamlet* was a regular feature but over the years devotees would have heard extracts from *Richard II, The Two Gentlemen of Verona* and *Troilus and Cressida*, plays rarely or never performed in the professional theatre. In 1877 the trapping of Parolles and the wooing of Diana (no doubt suitably bowdlerised) in *All's Well that Ends Well* were presented.

However, when the all-male Society occasionally staged fund-raising single performances of full-scale production, the event usually conformed to traditional expectations. In 1876 at the Prince of Wales Theatre, a benefit performance of *The Merchant of Venice* for the manager Walter Raynham (who played Shylock), ended with the trial scene while time was found for a pantomime of *Gulliver's Travels*. At the same theatre in 1878, a farce *A Grateful Father*

19

augmented a performance of *Macbeth* staged with Locke's music and the appearance of Hecate. In 1880 at the Holte Theatre in Aston Lower Grounds, Hamlet was played by W. T. Bennett 'author of *Shakespeare from a Builder's Point of View*', in what was claimed to be the first performance of the play ever seen in Aston. But there was no Fortinbras (which was usual in nineteenth-century production) and Osric was played by Miss Jessie Villars. As with a performance of *Othello* staged at the Theatre Royal in aid of the Shakespeare Library fund in 1879, professional actresses were engaged for the female roles. The press notices were tactfully sympathetic about the physically and vocally inept amateurs.

For more prestigious professional performance of Shakespeare, Birmingham audiences, along with the majority of provincial playgoers, had to rely on touring companies with visiting stars. While Birmingham could boast that it was creating one of the finest Shakespeare libraries in the country, there was no permanent, resident theatre company to recreate the texts on the stage. London-based actor–managers dominated the production values of Shakespeare as indeed they always had, except that by the 1880s the situation was if anything more problematic because of the demise of the provincial stock companies. Birmingham, at any rate during the 1840s and 50s before standards declined, had sustained relatively high quality support for visiting leading actors. But there was no denying the drawing power of the star actors. The programme books for the Prince of Wales, the Grand and the Theatre Royal bear witness to the regular opportunities for Birmingham audiences to see Herbert Beerbohm Tree, Lewis Waller, Johnston Forbes-Robertson, Oscar Asche, Martin-Harvey and (perhaps pre-eminently in the 1880s and early 1890s), Henry Irving, partnered by Ellen Terry. Each tour would include not only one or two Shakespearian plays, but also the romantic dramas which audiences loved and actor–managers could bank on. In 1891 at the Prince of Wales Irving and Terry showed their most enduring individual vehicles, *The Bells* and *Nance Oldfield*, in repertoire with *The Merchant of Venice*. Sixteen years later in 1907 Oscar Asche would draw huge audiences at the Theatre Royal for a programme based on the same formula. His West End productions of *Othello* and *The Taming of the Shrew* with Lily Brayton as Desdemona and Katharine were teamed with Rudolph Besier's *The Virgin Goddess*. The provinces, according to Drinkwater in his autobiography *Discovery*, were 'kindled . . . to a flame of play-going ardour'. He remembered the fury of applause 'a succession of calls, and an astonished leading actor protesting that in no city of the kingdom were his unworthy efforts so magnanimously supported'.[5] Certainly Irving at his best could mesmerise audiences, stamping the indelible impression of Lyceum Shakespeare on a whole generation of theatre-goers. In 1927, John Drinkwater gave an account of an attempt to see Irving on tour in Birmingham at the Prince of Wales Theatre. He described pleading for one of the ninepenny metal tokens which gained him admission into the over-crowded gallery:

> After furtive and vain efforts to squeeze myself into some corner of vantage, I somehow climbed up the back wall, swarmed along a beam on my stomach and lay the entire evening in a six inch accumulation of dust, peering down from the roof on to a stage that seemed to be a mile away. And I would, if I could, do the same thing again tonight in order to see Henry Irving act.[6]

We can only speculate about how often Barry Jackson attended the theatre in London, although his extensive childhood travels in Europe, including eighteen months in Geneva studying French at the age of sixteen, suggest there would have been ample opportunity to spend an evening at the Lyceum or Her Majesty's. The memories assembled in 1955 for an article 'Producing the Comedies'[7] provide evidence for considerable experience and enjoyment of actor–managers' Shakespeare. But he also recalled how the scene change from the trial scene to the final sequence in Belmont in Irving's *The Merchant of Venice* took twenty minutes while the orchestra played the major part of Luigini's *Egyptian Ballet* in order, Jackson claimed, 'to encourage conversation'. He was 'a trifle astonished' by Orsino's serenade to Olivia in Augustine Daly's 1894 'Rearrangement of Shakespeare's *Twelfth Night*' which came with Ada Rehan as Viola to the Theatre Royal in 1897. In addition to transforming Schubert's *Who is Sylvia?* to *Who is Olivia?* Daly also included a chorus of villagers in the sea-coast set which opened the play, singing Purcell's *Come unto these Yellow Sands*. Jackson, too, was dazzled

21

by Tree's excesses in *Twelfth Night*: the multiple Malvolios and the gorgeous garden set with its descending terraces, grass and fountains. He may well have seen the full splendour of the production in London. In a letter to J. C. Trewin in 1959, Jackson also recalled Tree's Hamlet on tour 'deplorable at the Birmingham Theatre Royal with scenery which must have served the Muddlecomb amateurs'.[8] Not only did the touring system mean the possibility of stale or second-rate production values, but there was a lack of opportunities for provincial scenic artists other than those provided by locally-produced pantomime.

There were some provincial managers who attempted homegrown spectacular Shakespeare. Jackson's 1955 article refers to Edward Saker who carried on the tradition in Liverpool; and while he does not mention the name of Richard Flanagan, he does describe in some detail the scenic orgies perpetrated by him in Manchester. From 1896 at the Queeen's Theatre, Flanagan staged (with his own designs), a series of richly extravagant and hugely popular revivals of Shakespeare. John Drinkwater, temporarily enslaved in insurance in Manchester, was as enthralled as the rest of the population. In *Discovery* he described seeing two of Flanagan's revivals — *Romeo and Juliet* (1905) and *Cymbeline* (1906) — six times each. Harcourt Williams, who played Romeo, later recalled sixteen weeks of houses packed with mill-hands and city workers avid for colour and romance. Indeed Williams was astonished, after exiting from the balcony scene, to see Flanagan onstage, bowler hat in hand, acknowledging applause for the set.[9] The Manchester productions regularly played for several weeks in Birmingham. Jackson may well have seen the live bear introduced into *The Winter's Tale* when it appeared on the stage of the Theatre Royal in September 1911. There were live deer in the Flanagan *As You Like It*. A few months before his own production of *Twelfth Night* Jackson could have enjoyed Flanagan's version. The long list of scene locations began with 'The Wreck' and finished with the grand tableau of the marriage of Viola and the Duke of Illyria. Jackson described an ending in 'true pantomime tradition — a general entrance, a double marriage ceremony in the Illyrian cathedral'.[10]

Jackson's first experience of seeing professional Shakespeare performance, however, had been Frank Benson's touring production of *The Taming of the Shrew* when it came to the Theatre Royal in 1889. Three years earlier Benson had been asked to become director of the annual Shakespeare Festival at Stratford-upon-Avon, a responsibility he maintained until 1919. Not only did Benson bring one of his touring companies annually to Birmingham but the geographical proximity of Birmingham to Stratford meant that Jackson owed most of his early Shakespearian theatre-going to Benson. Jackson was born just a few months after Charles Flower opened the first Shakespeare Memorial Theatre in a fantastical Gothic/Elizabethan building in Stratford on 23 April 1879. The visual absurdity of the building and the scaled-down versions of actor–manager's Shakespeare which were staged during each festival belied the genuinely radical ideas of the founder. A voracious reader of Shakespeare and champion of the lesser known plays, Charles Flower was fired by a dream to use his wealth to create a privately subsidised company conducted on the lines of the Meiningen Court Theatre Company, which even before its highly influential visit to London in 1881 was celebrated in Europe for its democratically organised ensemble playing of Shakespeare. Benson's claim that he ran his company on 'Meiningen principles' was his chief attraction for Flower, but at heart Benson was an actor–manager of the Irving school. He had a preference for the traditionally limited range of Shakespeare's plays — Irving's fame rested on the production of only twelve — and his policy of focusing interest on the central (or the most rewarding) character meant casting and cutting the texts in the time-honoured manner. By the turn of the century, when Benson still had aspirations to become another Irving, he was regarded in some circles as little more than a joke, especially after Max Beerbohm's wickedly funny review of Benson's disastrous Lyceum season in 1900.[11]

However, as Jackson pointed out 'Spectacle was not Benson's strong suit'.[12] The exigencies of touring and chronic financial problems compelled him to be less scenically lavish. The need to split the company into groups to tour different parts of the country and the annual commitment to the Stratford Festival turned the Bensonians into a well-trained and disciplined company capable of an unusual degree of ensemble playing. In 1900 the eminent scholar Sidney Lee defended Benson. While acknowledging the manager's shortcomings, Lee believed that his twenty-four years of almost total devotion to Shakespeare had laid the foundations for an ideal company where actors could be trained and 'the perpetual iteration of Shakespeare's words could be permanently secured'.[13]

Furthermore the Flower family compelled Benson to stage at least one unfamiliar Shakespearian play each season. In 1906, Archibald Flower, the son of Charles Flower, persuaded Benson to stage the *Henry VI* trilogy, his father's favourite plays. When Jackson saw these heavily cut and telescoped performances the seed was sown for his own famous productions of them nearly half a century later. With the exception of *Titus Andronicus*, which had to wait for Peter Brook's 1955 production, John Coleman's notorious 1900 *Pericles* (of which Jackson had hilarious memories of the elderly star's seaweed-strewn pink fleshings) and Poel's *Measure for Measure* and *Troilus and Cressida* in 1908 and 1913, Benson staged the entire canon. He even included a two-day full text of *Hamlet* in 1899 which Jackson also saw. Perhaps most important for young theatregoers like Jackson and Drinkwater, Benson's productions were exciting. Drinkwater wrote 'he was never flat or dull or little . . . Under his spell things happened, communications were made, beacons and furnaces were lit, the veritable soul of Shakespeare took the boards.'[14] In 1920 the eighteen-year old Ralph Richardson saw the ageing Benson play Hamlet in Brighton and heard him, in response to the Ghost, scrape his drawn sword on the stage making a weird spine-chilling noise. Richardson remembered the emotion it generated: 'if only I could be an actor, if only I could have a sword and scratch it on the floor, I wouldn't want to do anything else'.[15] Within four years, Richardson was a member of the Birmingham Repertory Company.

Twenty years before, in the late spring of 1904 it was a Bensonian, H. O. Nicholson, who took charge of a production of scenes from *Twelfth Night* played in the garden of Jackson's family home at The Grange in Moseley and subsequently in the grounds of the asylum in Knowle. Nicholson played Aguecheek — a role he frequently performed with Benson, while Jackson played Feste. Malvolio was performed by a wealthy young insurance clerk, Herbert Stowell Milligan, who introduced John Drinkwater into Jackson's circle of friends. Drinkwater was immediately given the part of Fabian. C. R.

(Tim) Dawes, another rich and erudite young man who had persuaded Nicholson to assist the Birmingham amateurs, played Sir Toby Belch. At that first meeting Drinkwater also met the father whose entrepreneurial zeal had created the Maypole Dairy Company from a small shop in the Bull Ring and noted that despite the arthritis which now confined him to a wheelchair George Jackson had high hopes of his son's theatrical enthusiasm. Certainly the man who had run away from his own father did not compel Barry Jackson to follow his elder brother into the business, or continue the training as an architect in the office of Frank Osborn which had proved scarcely tolerable for five years. The library in The Grange was enlarged with dramatic literature and rooms set aside for the pursuit of theatre.

Barry Jackson had enjoyed all the social and educational benefits of great wealth. Taught by a private tutor after preparatory school, he spoke several languages, had nursed dreams of becoming a painter and had first-hand experience of European culture and theatre. Drinkwater's background could not have been more different. At 22, two years younger than Jackson, he had suffered vicariously the harsher aspects of the theatrical life. His father A. E. Drinkwater had abandoned teaching for a prolonged and only intermittently successful struggle to earn a stable living as an actor and dramatist. He had directed the first financially disastrous provincial tour of Shaw's *Arms and the Man* and had played Marchbanks in the copyright performance of *Candida* in South Shields in 1895. He was thus the kind of actor who would have benefited most from the professional reforms represented by the repertory movement. As it was he became Secretary of the Stage Society and manager of the Little and Kingsway Theatres in London for Granville Barker and Lillah McCarthy and was later Jackson's London representative. In 1898, however, A. E. was adamant, despite tears and protestations, that his son should enter a secure profession. Jackson at sixteen was in Geneva attending the opera and French light comedy. At the same age Drinkwater became a junior clerk in the Northern Assurance Company in Nottingham, existing on what were almost literally starvation wages. By the time he met Jackson, Drinkwater had experienced not only the first stirrings of literary ambition, but also an acute consciousness of the

25

inadequacy of his early education.

The 1904 performance yielded the first surviving photographic record of Jackson's amateur Shakespeare: an entertaining romp in a beautiful Edwardian garden with Miss Grace Garbutt as Viola in a costume very like the one worn on the Rep first night and Jackson in an extraordinary parti-coloured jagged tunic and coxcomb jester's cap. Programmes exist for other earlier performances of the play: in February at the Birmingham School of Art, where Jackson had also studied, and for another garden showing at The Grange in June 1903. Jackson and his friends at this stage were doing little more than following on a tradition for family theatricals which dated back to long before he was born. It is obvious, however, from Drinkwater's memoirs that Jackson had aspirations for something more ambitious but as yet this was ill-defined. There is now no trace of the early plays Jackson wrote, though Drinkwater took part in *Blinkin' Bill, A Farce in Three Acts, by B.V.J.* performed before an invited audience at The Grange for Christmas 1904. Although Drinkwater states that he was forced to leave Birmingham for Manchester in January 1905, there is a programme for a garden performance of scenes from *As You Like It* the following June when Jackson played Orlando and Drinkwater the banished Duke. There are no obvious signs in these isolated ventures that the Birmingham group felt themselves to be part of a radical movement which was beginning to gather momentum across the country. Open-air productions of Shakespeare, especially the popular comedies where outdoor locations are integral to the action, had first been made consistently available by the actor–manager Ben Greet when he formed his Woodland Players in 1886. A collection of programmes in Jackson's personal archive bear witness to regular performances of Shakespeare in Birmingham's Botanical Gardens by both Greet's and Benson's companies. One programme is of special interest in view of Jackson's future ventures. In July 1901 a company bearing the names of E. Harcourt Williams (then a young Bensonian) and Garnet Holme, brought a production of the rarely-staged *The Two Gentlemen of Verona* to the Botanical Gardens. Williams played Valentine to the Proteus of Leon Quartermaine while H. O. Nicholson played Speed. Each change of location was heralded by the sounding of a gong. In an age of stage-realism, real trees and hedges in Shakespeare's fictive woods and gardens were seen as highly appropriate and of course, then as now, outdoor performance can be a practical and economic method of play production for both professionals and amateurs.

In some circles, by the turn of the century, amateur theatricals had begun to acquire an almost evangelical respectability. Proponents of reform like Poel or Edward Gordon Craig used groups of amateurs to conduct staging experiments which would have been impossible in the professional theatre. In fact the individual eccentricities of both meant that neither could ever work satisfactorily within a commercial context. Also, aspiring professional artists — Harley Granville Barker, who played Richard II and Edward II for Poel, is just one striking example — were drawn into amateur projects which would later bear fruit in attempts to reform mainstream theatre. But inevitably amateur experiment was obscure and confined to a few performances with limited audiences. Poel's co-production with Ben Greet of *Everyman* was his only venture which made money. When it was staged at the Midland Institute in 1902 as part of a tour of provincial cities, it gave Jackson his first opportunity to see Poel's work. Poel was distressed that this popular success came from the revival of a medieval morality rather than an Elizabethan play. But the impressive austerity of the performances and the references in costume and the positioning of the actors to Italian Renaissance painting of religious subjects created an effect which was both harmonious and simple. Apparently Craig hated the play 'because it was so against all I believe, but people loved it and it was mighty powerful'.[16] For Jackson and his friends in 1907, another early morality *The Interlude of Youth*, found in Dodsley's collection of old plays in Jackson's library, proved an ideal subject for their modest experiments in simplified staging.

The first public performance of *The Interlude of Youth* by the newly named Pilgrim Players took place on 2 October 1907 in the Mission Hall in Inge Street in the parish of St Jude, the worst slum district in Birmingham. The vicar, Arnold Pinchard, was one of a growing number of clerics who had come to see the theatre as a force for good within society and it was he who had invited Poel to bring *Everyman* to Birmingham. High Anglican worship in the parish became vigorously theatrical on religious festival days, when

Pinchard, dressed in full liturgical robes, led his choir in procession through the streets with the cross held high. An excellent horseman and amateur boxer who had spent the early part of his ministry in the Falkland Islands, he was quite capable of knocking out any jeering bystander. Pinchard was in the audience for the initial performance of *Youth* at The Grange and after issuing the invitation to the group to perform at St Jude's refused to use the event for charitable purposes. He wanted the play and the company to succeed on their own merits. Subsequently Pinchard directed several of the Pilgrim productions, including *King John* and *Measure for Measure*, as well as four plays during the first year of the new theatre.

Bache Matthews, later to become Business Manager of the Rep, as well as its first historian, was in the audience for *Youth*. A few weeks later Drinkwater invited him to join an augmented cast for E. A. Buckton's modern miracle play *Eager Heart*. Drinkwater described Matthews as a small, quiet clerk in the Corporation water works 'But he had a passion for Elizabethan literature especially dramatic literature and people with a passion were what we wanted'.[17] When Matthews protested that he had little acting ability, Drinkwater cheerfully assured him that acting experience was of less importance than a serious interest in good drama. Subsequently in 1911 the obvious lack of expertise in acting and directing, especially in modern drama, provoked some sharp comment from F. A. Besant Rice, then the dramatic critic of the *Birmingham Daily Post*. Rice had learnt the art of effective stage production while working as private secretary to the arch-perfectionist Arthur Wing Pinero. He now offered the benefits of his experience to the Pilgrims and after a successful production of St. John Hankin's *Return of the Prodigal* continued to direct for the Company until 1915.

On 16 December 1907, just before the first performance of *Eager Heart*, an article appeared in the *Birmingham Daily Post* setting out the general aims of the Pilgrim Players. This lengthy statement gave an account of the development of the provincial repertory movement and made it clear that the Pilgrims saw themselves as part of that movement: 'whose definite object it is to put before the Birmingham public such plays that cannot be seen in the ordinary way . . . Their attention will, for the most part, be confined to old English plays, but considerable catholicity will be observed in the matter of selection'. The general seriousness of the project was further emphasised by the fact that they would remain anonymous. Of course, as the memoirs of Matthews and Drinkwater reveal, the activities of the Pilgrims were not all so high-minded. There was a good deal of enjoyment in amateur playmaking. But a highly disciplined regime of rehearsal and planning was quickly established and the Pilgrims were soon able to select only the best out of any possible candidates for the group. These earnest young people were like missionaries:

> Those rehearsals in a shoddy little upstair room, loud not with the murmur of bees but with the clatter of corporation trams, were preparations for the Kingdom. To hear a commercial traveller, an iron merchant, an auctioneer's clerk, a lawyer, and a tailor, all of them young in the competitive commerce of a great industrial city, transfigured by the verse of Shakespeare or Yeats . . . was to realise that here were men to whom a call had come[18]

As in Liverpool where leading intellectuals sponsored the development of the repertory theatre, members of Birmingham's cultural élite supported the company: men like Charles Gore the city's first bishop, Whitworth Wallis, Keeper of the Art Gallery, Oliver Lodge, Principal of the University (granted its Royal Charter in 1900) and Ernest de Selincourt who held the Chair of English. De Selincourt, active in the formation of a Birmingham Playgoer's Society, consciously aimed to educate opinion towards the establishment of a local repertory theatre which Jackson and his colleagues would control. At the end of 1909 Jackson enabled Drinkwater to give up his promising career in insurance and use his undoubted charm and powers of persuasion in the interests of the new venture. Over a period of five years, a total of twenty-eight plays were produced including *Everyman*; *Deirdre* and *The King's Threshold* by Yeats; *The Silver Box* by Galsworthy; Ibsen's *An Enemy of the People*; *Press Cuttings* and *How He Lied to Her Husband* by Shaw; and two by Drinkwater himself: *Cophetua*, his first attempt at verse drama, and a pantomime *Puss in Boots*. There were three Shakespearian plays: *The Two Gentlemen of Verona*, *Measure for Measure* and *King John*. In June 1910, at the request of W. B. Yeats, the Company gave three performances of *The King's Threshold* at the Court Theatre in London. Yeats, who had written to Drinkwater on the publication of *Lyrical and Other Poems* in 1909, came in April 1910 to see and praise *Measure for Measure*. In London, however, the Pilgrims suffered from the antagonism of the Irish Players with whom they shared the theatre. As Drinkwater readily admitted, the amateurs had great difficulty with the 'sustained external immobility of Yeats's lyric drama'.[19] By 1912, the group was calling itself the Birmingham Repertory Company and members were paid a small salary by Jackson.

When *The Two Gentlemen of Verona* was staged in April 1908 the cold, dingy Inge Street Mission was abandoned in favour of the Edgbaston Assembly Rooms, which became a permanent home during the amateur years. In 1921 Jackson recalled the move from the slum parish hall to the affluent area of Edgbaston. It would have been easy, he suggested, to form a large popular audience from the poorer working people: 'This type of audience, as is proved by the experiment at the Old Vic, loves its Shakespeare, its Opera, loves vigorous action and colour'.[20] Jackson, rather like Matthew Arnold and William Archer half a century before, wanted to break the indifference and philistinism of the middle classes. In 1889 in 'A Plea for an Endowed Theatre' Archer, borrowing a phrase from Ibsen, advocated the creation of audiences who would form a 'compact majority' for non-commercial plays that would appeal to 'the thousands, not to the tens of thousands'.[21] Ideally this élite would then educate the greater, less discriminating majority. It was an understandable but dangerous wish. As the new kind of theatre struggled into existence, a cultural divide began to open up which was to create serious problems. As we have already seen, the Birmingham Repertory Theatre could adopt a deliberately non-popularist policy because Barry Jackson was able to supply a financial safety net. Jackson set himself to oppose the practice of giving the audience 'what it wants'. It was, he stated, the function of the new leaders in the theatre to change public taste. It was necessary to give 'the public what it ought to have, and what given the opportunity it will slowly begin to demand as it wakes to new and hitherto undreamed of possibilities'.[22] Certainly when the Rep opened there was every effort to ensure a widely diverse audience. The physical and social structure of commercial late-Victorian theatre with its expensive stalls, boxes and dress circles tended to reinforce a rigidly stratified society, whereas the democratic sweep of the Rep's seating represented something of a social revolution. After the first night several critics expressed surprise at the cheapness of the seats. When prices were raised in 1917 and a ticket voucher system introduced, representations were made by the Workers' Educational Association and cheaper 'privilege tickets' were issued for certain performances and distributed to various institutions including factory welfare centres. But as Jackson was to discover in the years to come, Birmingham people would not always accept what they 'ought to have'. The Shakespeare revolution, which Jackson and his friends helped to lead, inevitably destroyed even as it recreated. Much of the popular appeal of old-style Shakespeare which packed provincial theatres while Jackson was a boy would vanish.

The revolution itself, however, was part of a complex evolutionary process which had begun to affect all the arts in Europe by the end of the nineteenth century. The Pilgrim Players' first Shakespeare experiments were shaped by forces seeking to transform the aesthetic and technical basis of British theatre as a whole. The next chapter will explore the influences which led the Pilgrims to the staging methods which would become essential to the Rep's long-term policy on Shakespeare production.

Chapter Three
The First Pilgrim Experiments: 1904–1912

The elaborate pictorial stage settings and careful reconstruction of historical period which characterised late Victorian Shakespeare production, and which were subsequently challenged during the Edwardian decade, were the result of an attempt to bring a greater sense of physical and psychological realism into theatrical experience. With Irving, for example, the picture-stage acquired an artistic unity of remarkable beauty and sophistication, not least because he employed celebrated artists and highly skilled scene-painters to design and execute his sets and costumes. The total visual effect at the Lyceum, enhanced by the subtle glow of gas stage lighting, could be stunning. But the picture-stage remained obstinately two-dimensional, merely a painted background for the action, rather than a three-dimensional environment peopled by living actors. The introduction of electric stage lighting in the early 1880s exacerbated the feeling of frustration by revealing the essential tawdriness of painted canvas back-cloths, cut-cloths and sky borders. Painted shadows and perspective became ridiculous and the intensity of the illumination from footlights and proscenium-frame lights cast real shadows which obscured the actor's face and induced a ghastly pallor. To achieve the semblance of reality, the new technology had to complement three-dimensional settings without sacrificing the capacity of gas lighting to heighten mood and atmosphere.

In the theatre of modern naturalistic drama which required the scenic effect of plausible domesticity, the use of realistic, solidly-built and furnished box-sets had been gathering momentum since Madam Vestris's innovations in the 1830s. Also, the nineteenth-century enthusiasm for classical Greek and Roman art which spawned new plays such as Tennyson's *The Cup* and W. G. Wills's *Claudian* created interest in classical and Renaissance theatre, where a stage was an architectural space through which the actor moved to communicate with his audience. Edward Gordon Craig's father, E. W. Godwin, was not only an artist, archaeologist and designer but also a distinguished architect. His attempts in both written theory and practice to achieve artistic unity in minutely researched, historically precise stage settings and costumes helped to influence the massively accurate settings for the Bancrofts' 1875 *The Merchant of Venice*, and later resulted in the spectacular Byzantine designs for Wilson Barrett's 1883 production of *Claudian* and the designs for John Todhunter's *Helena in Troas*, staged in the indoor amphitheatre of Hengler's Circus. Barry Jackson saw (probably in 1891) a late touring version of Wilson Barrett's *Hamlet* with Godwin's 1884 designs. In 1959 Jackson remembered the unusually subtle idea of setting the play scene in an orchard.[1] The twelve-year old Jackson clearly recognised a scenic innovation but probably not its technical significance. Godwin was attempting in that scene to overcome the obligatory back-cloth in order to create real perspective and three-dimensional groupings. Also in the summer of 1884, a stage orchard was supplanted by an actual outdoor setting when the Pastoral Players, a group of aesthetically-minded amateurs and professionals under Godwin's direction, performed the woodland scenes from *As You Like It* in a grove of lime trees on an estate near to Coombe House in Kingston-upon-Thames. Pastoral Shakespeare, which Jackson was to find so useful in his earliest Shakespearian ventures, was for Godwin part of the quest for total realism.[2]

In the theatre itself the quest was self-defeating. By 1899, the first performance of Shakespeare on silent film (Tree in *King John*) was pointing the way to which verisimilitude to life would be achieved. What was central to the new stagecraft was the realisation that simple suggestion could replace elaborate representation. The rapid transition in art, at the turn of the century, from the depiction of naturalistic and narrative detail was prompted by the desire in Symbolism and Post-Impressionism to synthesise visual and emotional experience in the use of pure colour and simple emphatic

33

line. In 1921 Jackson summed up his approach to stage design (and here we must remember his apprentice days in the architect's office and his evenings at the School of Art): 'The high water mark of everything that is fined down and down is simplicity. To be complex and reach the desired result is the work of talent. To be simple and reach the same result is the work of genius'.[3] Edward Gordon Craig winnowed away the obssesive attention to detail which characterised the work of his two father figures, Godwin and Irving, to concentrate on the genius for artistic unity in form and colour which lay at the heart of their work. Also at the same time as Adolphe Appia was developing concepts of combining light with solid mass to promote a sense of emotional and psychological reality, Craig was taking over innovations in lighting devised for the pictorial stage to complement simplified, solid, three-dimensional settings where his actors could move as in a real environment. Craig witnessed the experiments of the society painter Hubert von Herkomer, who staged amateur productions in his private theatre between 1889 and 1890 which abolished footlights and introduced carefully positioned overhead and auditorium lighting. His realistically convincing 'stage moon', accompanied by subtle colour changes, proved it was possible to simulate sky effects without recourse to painted canvas.[4] In Craig's productions with amateurs between 1899 and 1902, a lighting bridge above the stage and the projectors at the back of the auditorium shone light on to plain-coloured cloths which draped both the stage and the auditorium, achieving an impression of harmony and spaciousness.

In 1955 Jackson, with the help of his long-established designer Paul Shelving, tried to recall the impact of Craig's 1903 production of *Much Ado about Nothing* which came on tour to the Prince of Wales Theatre in Birmingham:

> Here was that impressive simplicity of scenic design that is achieved only by means of impeccable taste. It consisted of three full sets and a frontcloth for intermediary scenes. The Church Scene was a miracle of beauty that I have never seen surpassed . . . Shelving recalls a flickering of buildings in the Pent-house Scene, and I remember a horizontal shaft of light . . . which could not possibly have emanated from the front of the auditorium as it would have caused shadows.[5]

The contents of Jackson's library show that he was familiar with Craig's published theories. Although Craig habitually thought and designed on a grand scale, his emphasis on simple beauty and utility which employed very basic materials could be easily adapted to the needs of the new small theatres. The use of a single scenic feature or architectural framework served to focus and stimulate the audience's imagination. In Volume Four of *The Mask* Craig's description of an ideal evocation of the Doge's palace in Venice might be a formula for one of Jackson's sets in the Rep's early years: 'By one rich pillar, by some projecting balustrade taken in conjunction with a moored gondola, we should strive to evoke the soul of the city of Veronese'.[6] Furthermore, Jackson not only deployed the concept of simplicity and suggestiveness in Shakespeare production but in all the poetic drama for which he provided designs in the Rep's early years.

Craig also knew that colour could capture the essence of a play. In 1911 he described a design for *Macbeth* where he envisaged two basic elements: a rock and the mist surrounding it and only two principal colours: 'Touch not a single other colour, but only those two colours through your whole progress of designing your scene and your costume. Yet forget not that each colour contains many variations'.[7] In 1920 after the subtle evocative use of colour had become a particular feature of Jackson's design practice and of Rep Shakespeare, Jackson warned, 'Colour and pattern are capable of ruining plays and players . . . Directly the eye is drawn hither and thither about the scene — puzzled by the complexity of pattern . . . the spirit of the play evaporates'. He recalled seeing Eleonora Duse (the Italian actress famed for the expressiveness of her face) perform in front of a stock scene in a French provincial theatre: 'It may be that I am peculiarly sensitive to pattern but the horrible panels of pink and green and blue scrolls; the gilden scanthus [sic] leaves wandering around the frieze are more vivid in memory than the Duse herself'.[8] Ultimately the complex language and characterisation of Shakespeare's plays and even the human actor would seem irrelevant to Craig's ideal scene: a synthesis of sound, movement, form and colour. For Jackson, just as it was important that no actor should dominate the play itself, so no setting should overwhelm the actor.

The early Pilgrim performances inevitably capitalised on their primary resources: the plays and the commitment of the actors. In 1924 Bache Matthews described how *The Interlude of Youth* began with a procession of actors led by acolytes swinging censers and carrying tapers: 'The verse was spoken clearly and with conviction; no unnecessary gestures were used, and there was none of the fidgetiness that is frequently so irritating in the performance of amateur actors'.[9] An unseen choir sang Arcadelt's *Ave Maria* and processional hymns while the setting, on an open platform, consisted of bright green curtains hung in a semi-circle with three entrances labelled 'The World', 'The Citie of Blyss' and 'The Tavern'. At least one review remembered Poel's *Everyman* and evidently the small audiences found an impressive power in the moral certainties of the play and the dignity of the actors. It was all very different to the kind of amateur performance which Birmingham had endured in the past. By the following year, however, as the company prepared to tackle Shakespeare again, a clearly defined agenda began to emerge.

On 21 April 1908, a week before the Pilgrims' first performance of *The Two Gentlemen of Verona* at the Edgbaston Assembly Rooms, John Drinkwater published an article on 'The Draped Stage' in the *Birmingham Daily Mail*, preparing the city for what he obviously thought was a daring experiment. The man who two years before had been spell-bound by Flanagan's lavish realism argued that representational scenery rarely or never succeeded in creating total illusion: 'People will tell you that it is the business of the stage to put before the audience a picture of life both in its action and its background and that the rejection of scenery is a voluntary handicap in this purpose'. Drinkwater insisted that it was the purpose of poetic drama not to represent life, but to interpret it. Shakespeare wrote about the inner lives of men: 'all men at all time . . . action and time and place are in themselves of secondary importance . . . the smallest possible faculty of imagination will fashion for all the requisite detail and trappings, and to much more purpose than can paint and pasteboard'.

As Carey Mazer has demonstrated, the use of a stage draped with plain-coloured or tapestry-style curtains for economical innovation in the production of Shakespeare acquired growing if marginal currency during the Edwardian decade.[10] Beginning in the 1890s

Charles Fry's Shakespearean Company presented a series of 'costume recitals' of Shakespeare using beautiful costumes displayed to advantage against plain dark green curtains. Fry, who from 1885 was Professor of Elocution and Dramatic Art at the Hampstead Conservatoire of Music, used the popularity of dramatic recitals to bring Shakespeare to the slums of Bethnal Green where his company performed in unconventional venues which ranged from swimming baths to workers' centres. Between 1904 and 1908 there were also performances at the Court, Savoy and Kingsway Theatres. A few palms suggested forest or rural scenes and furniture was introduced as needed. Apart from one interval in the middle of the performance there were only brief pauses between each scene, where the stage was left bare. Poel was a devoted follower of Fry's work and the actors who benefited from an alternative scenic perspective and a splendid vocal training included Elsie Fogerty and Lewis Casson.[11] As a method for mainstream theatre, it was of course too austere. Beerbohm Tree boasted of his tapestried *Hamlet* for his first Shakespeare Festival in 1905, but the curtains were originally 'hung to prejudice, not to conviction' for practical touring reasons rather than as part of a sustained enterprise.[12] For the Birmingham group, however, staging a rarely performed play in virtually full text, it was an ideal preliminary move.

During March 1908 the Pilgrims prepared and painted six scenic canvas curtains, each 28 feet by 16 feet, which bore designs copied by Jackson from Carpaccio's *Legend of St Ursula*. These same curtains provided the tapestries for interior scenes in the 1913 *Twelfth Night* and they were still in use in 1924. Some critics in 1913 objected to the vivid colours — as well they might have done if the original had been accurately reproduced. However, Bache Matthews recorded that the costumes for *Two Gentlemen* were brighter than the curtains, which had been deliberately painted in softer hues to represent old tapestry. According to the programme the costumes were based on those painted by 'Lorenzo di Viterbo in 1469 in his fresco of the Sposalizio in the church of S. Maria della Verità, Viterbo'. Apart from a photograph of Margaret Chatwin, who read Drinkwater's birthday ode to Shakespeare, the only photographs that survive are of the men, including Jackson and Drinkwater as Valentine and Proteus. These individual portraits show elegant and accurate

37

fifteenth-century tunics and tabards with slashed sleeves, ornamental chains, caps and hats. Some reviews of the production compared the costumes to the exquisitely coloured and embroidered garments depicted in William Holman Hunt's picture *The Two Gentlemen of Verona – Valentine Rescuing Silvia from Proteus* in Birmingham Art Gallery. Poel, as we have already seen, habitually based his costumes on contemporary fifteenth and sixteenth-century pictures. A child brought up at the height of the Pre-Raphaelite movement, Poel was painted by Hunt as the boy Jesus in his *Discovery of Christ in the Temple* which was also part of the Birmingham gallery's collection. The introduction by George Brandes to the pocket-sized text of the play used as a prompt-book by the Pilgrims linked Shakespeare's gauche experiment in lyric comedy to the Brotherhood's high-minded romanticism: 'In almost every utterance of the young women in this comedy we see nobility of soul and in the lyric passages a certain Pre-Raphaelite grace'.[13] Just as Birmingham, like Manchester, had acquired a collection of art which seemed to represent the antithesis of its bustling industrial base, so the Pilgrims' choice of this play — ineptly-plotted and without obvious starring roles — was a direct challenge to the priorities of commercial theatre.

As the Birmingham reviews commented, *The Two Gentlemen* was rarely performed despite that fleeting visit to the Botanical Gardens in 1901. Benson himself did not stage the play until 1911. Indeed the lukewarm reception of Augustin Daly's production at his London theatre in 1895 (staged and adapted primarily to give Ada Rehan yet another starring opportunity) signalled the decline of his influence in the West End. But in a small way the play had become associated with the theatrical avant-garde. Poel's first production, given two performances in the winter of 1896/7, was both inaudible and monotonous but Lugné-Poë, the champion of new poetic and symbolist drama in the French theatre, saw it and recorded how Poel used the unconventional playing space of the Merchant Taylors' Hall: actors moved through the audience to create the effect of the journeys, escape and chase which are part of the narrative.[14] Harcourt Williams' troupe must have consciously chosen the play for its rarity value and indeed may well have sown the seed for the Pilgrim production. The use of the gong at the Botanical Gardens to signal change in location was another interesting, if modest attempt to reconcile the audience to the lack of representational scenery. Three years later in 1904 Granville Barker used *The Two Gentlemen* as a bargaining chip, agreeing to direct it at the Court (and play Speed) only if he could also stage six *Candida* matinées as well. The Barker–Vedrenne management at the Court and Shaw's subsequent success were born out of Shakespeare's unregarded juvenilia.

The immediate result of the Pilgrims' production was not so momentous but the fidelity to the play and the overall intelligence of the acting was generally admired. The treatment of the text was important at a time when radicals like Shaw, valuing words more than spectacle, inveighed against the traditional disembowelling of Shakespeare's plays — a practice reinforced by the published acting versions which cut minor characters indiscriminately and rearranged the scene order to accommodate set changes. The fact that the Pilgrims were able to use a pocket-sized edition of *The Two Gentlemen* based on the complete Cambridge text was a significant product of recent scholarship. Only some twenty lines were cut. The exact nature of Crab's misdemeanour in Lady Silvia's dining room was omitted and Proteus's threat to rape Silvia was modified by the removal of 'and love you 'gainst the nature of love — force ye' and 'I'll force thee yield to my desire' which also would allow the company to sidestep the problems of the play's dénouement. The *Birmingham Daily Mail* (28 April 1908) was generous in its praise of the standard of performance and took particular note of the virtually full text and the prominence given to the minor roles. The *Birmingham Pictorial* was a little more critical of the anonymous actors. Jackson as Valentine was 'unduly sonorous' and Drinkwater as Proteus 'almost montonously melancholy'. A few of their scenes together were 'recited rather than acted'. However the writer praised Speed (T. Foden Flint) and Launce (Bache Matthews). Silvia (Cecily Byrne) was 'endowed with much charm and maidenly simplicity', while Julia (Edythe Jones) was 'sufficiently sympathetic and seemed to derive inspiration from her boy's clothes'. Drinkwater's first wife, Cathleen Orford, played Lucetta.

Probably the production was little more than a dramatic recital on the Fry model, especially after Margaret Chatwin, in a heavily-draped classical robe, had read the birthday ode. The Edgbaston

Assembly Rooms held about 400 people and the small stage was lit by footlights and one top batten. Jackson removed the painted act-drop used as an all-purpose background, and had brown tableau curtains fitted behind the proscenium. The footlights were removed and two arc lamps, one on each side of the stage, provided the only illumination. The tapestry curtains completely enclosed the back and sides of the stage. After the ode the curtains parted to reveal a bust of Shakespeare displayed on a flight of four white steps half the width of the proscenium. Thereafter the steps did duty as Silvia's balcony and as a seat. Two stools supplied the only other furniture. The critic of the *Birmingham Pictorial* (1 May 1908) commented on the: 'soft yellow light radiating from the sides . . . particularly good was the transition from moonlight to sunshine, after the serenading of Silvia. This method of lighting, together with the curtains draping the stage gave quite a Gordon Craig effect, and was eminently suitable to the play'. The front curtain was not lowered during the performance but the ends of scenes were indicated by short pauses while the stage was left empty. Although Drinkwater had previously declared that 'action and time and place are in themselves of secondary importance' the programme does give a list of some twenty scene locations. Those pauses, however brief, must have interrupted the unlocalised flow of the original.

In 1955 Jackson described William Poel's 1903 production of *Measure for Measure*, seen in Stratford only a few days before the first performance of *The Two Gentlemen*, as his 'supreme awakening adventure': 'For the first time . . . I was caught up in the play's action, which divested of all the gallimaufrey on which I had been bred, rose triumphant, swift and sure . . . It was the text that mattered. Poel brushed aside all that interposed'.[15] Given that the Pilgrims' *The Two Gentlemen*, whatever its shortcomings, very decidedly brushed aside the 'gallimaufrey' of traditional productions, the septuagenarian Jackson may have been somewhat disingenuous. What Poel's work almost certainly did was to confirm the amateurs' objectives. In 1908 the Pilgrim programme announced a production of *All's Well that Ends Well* but in the event they staged *Measure for Measure* on 22 April 1910. Poel's production had used his permanent model of the Old Fortune Theatre, with an apron stage built out over the orchestra stalls of the Shakespeare Memorial

Theatre. The four acting areas: the apron, an inner stage split into two areas, and a balcony, were all divided by tapestry curtains. The Pilgrims wore Elizabethan costumes and in keeping with Poel's insistence that Isabella had not yet entered a religious order, Margaret Chatwin did not wear a nun's habit in the role. There was, however, no attempt to imitate Poel's reconstruction of an Elizabethan theatre. The Edgbaston stage was again draped with curtains, but instead of tapestries Jackson attempted some scenic suggestion with a combination of black curtains hung along the back and sides of the stage and a semi-circle of five grey curtains which evoked stone columns. The setting remained unaltered throughout the performance, with canvas-covered stools again serving as additional furniture. This time a synopsis of scene locations was considered unnecessary but the stage was still left empty for a few seconds after each scene — the effect of constant movement which the Poel production must have generated was disregarded.

It is ironic that Arnold Pinchard should have directed the production. Only two years before in Stratford, a clergyman had declared that *Measure for Measure* was not fit to be seen on the stage. But a long review in the *Birmingham Gazette* (23 April 1910) considered that '*Measure for Measure* is a strange play with great moments in it and one would gladly see it more often on the stage. It has been well said of it that of all Shakespeare's plays it comes nearer to any other to the direct discussion of a moral problem'. The writer then turned to the production itself:

> The simple drapery used by the Pilgrim Players was admirably chosen, as were the Elizabethan costumes worn. One would commend also the care with which they have prepared their version of the play. They have in no way distorted the action, they have not unduly clipped any of the characters in their version which should not offend the most sensitive taste.

No prompt-book has survived and so it is impossible to judge how the Pilgrims managed to mediate between distortion and offence. Robert Speaight's description of Poel's attempts to avoid the sexual explicitness of the original is an amusing account of high Victorian prudery confronting Elizabethan frankness.[16] In 1918 when the Rep company presented the play again there is evidence of considerable re-thinking as to what was, or was not, acceptable to post-war audiences.

In 1910 Margaret Chatwin's performance as Isabella was praised in several reviews with the *Birmingham Gazette* commending 'a very clever piece of restrained acting'. T. Foden Flint was a popular Lucio. But the *Gazette* complained that John Drinkwater's Angelo 'did not seem to be carried away by a sudden temptation but to be continually scheming. Some would think there was a little too much of the calculating hypocrite in the player's reading of the part'. Jackson as Vincentio gave an uneven performance punctuated with occasional fine speaking. Both the *Gazette* and the *Birmingham Mail* again praised the portrayal of the minor characters.

Shakespeare's minor characters had been among the chief casualties of actor–managers' Shakespeare. In 1922 Jackson spoke of the importance of retaining them in production: 'The more one sees of Shakespearean drama, the more important does the second senator, the captain, a messenger become. If a few lines are cut out or acted in a meaningless manner, the entire structure of the play falls like a pack of cards'.[17] It was a lesson well learnt from Poel. For all the apparent inconsistencies in his work, Poel's rigorous dismissal of traditional or sentimental notions about Shakespeare's characters and his insistence on the importance of looking at a text in its entirety and if possible in its original form was a vital contribution to twentieth-century production of Shakespeare. Robert Speaight's 1954 biography of Poel drew on a dossier of letters and recollections assembled by Jackson in 1948 for a proposed monograph.[18] When Jackson came to review Speaight's book in 1955 he referred to Poel's eccentricities, especially his habit of casting women in men's roles. But with reference to Poel's 1908 *Measure for Measure* he said: '. . . its treatment as far as continuity and rapidity are concerned has coloured the twenty-nine plays of the Shakespeare canon that have been produced at the Birmingham Repertory Theatre'.[19]

Certainly Poel's ideas surfaced in the Rep's productions. As in the Rep's 1913 *Twelfth Night*, Poel's 1903 Elizabethan Stage Society production of the play dressed Olivia and her household in black. When the childlike quality of Gwen Ffrangçon-Davies's Juliet was acknowledged as the most striking feature of the Rep's 1922 production it was recalled that Poel always emphasised the extreme youth of the two lovers. Poel also stressed the youth of Hamlet, a position that Jackson maintained until the end of his life. Indeed as we shall see there was a clear link between Poel and the modern-dress production of *Hamlet* in 1925. Modern-dress Shakespeare was the logical outcome of Poel's dream of creating a special kind of theatrical realism in which actor and audience could collaborate in a shared experience: something which no amount of representational scenery could achieve. In a letter replying to Poel's appraisal of the modern-dress *Hamlet* Jackson acknowledged his mentor: 'Whether you like it or not, I have always regarded you as one of my real godfathers in the world of the theatre'.[20]

Virtually everyone who admired Poel's theories set about translating them in terms of modern scenography. No one in Britain, until Nugent Monck founded the Maddermarket Theatre in Norwich in 1921, seriously contemplated Poel's reconstruction of an Elizabethan theatre. Recently Carey Mazer has demonstrated that Poel's belief in the use of traverse curtains on the Elizabethan platform stage to create localised zones for performance was no more than an attempt to utilise Victorian stagecraft using widely-held, but faulty scholarship as a justification.[21] But there can be no doubt that stage directors found the use of curtains an important aid in combining the deeply-rooted need for a certain degree of scenic representation with the provision of space for the actors and the free movement of the play. In December 1904 the French director André Antoine brought his production of *King Lear* to London where it was seen by Lewis Casson, then a member of Barker's Court company. This offered 'A permanent setting with complete continuity of action — the characters moving forward and tabs closing behind them for transition scenes, no act divisions — simply twenty-eight tableaux'.[22] In Manchester in 1909, the year after he had invited Poel to direct the repertory company in *Measure for Measure*, Ben Iden Payne staged *Much Ado About Nothing* at the Gaiety Theatre. The designer Hugh Fremantle used full sets which were pictorial representations of sixteenth-century Italy but short connecting scenes were played in front of neutral curtains. In 1910 Tree invited Poel to stage *The Two Gentlemen of Verona* for the sixth annual Shakespeare Festival at His Majesty's Theatre and allowed him to build an apron stage out over the orchestra pit and install front lighting from the balconies. The following year Tree retained both these innovations for his own *Henry VIII* (which again Jackson probably saw) but — outrageously — for a sumptuous production which lasted four hours despite the loss of the final act.

Earlier in the spring of 1911 Jackson devised a staging for Arnold Pinchard's Pilgrim production of *King John* which formed the basis for Rep Shakespeare design until after the Second World War. What Bache Matthews later described as the 'three-stage method' proved, once combined with the principles of the new stagecraft, to be an enduring compromise with the Elizabethanists. The method was exploited most spectacularly by Barker's Savoy productions of Shakespeare but it was also used regularly after the First World War at the Shakespeare Memorial Theatre and the Old Vic. At the Edgbaston Assembly Rooms in 1911 there was no possibility of building a forestage but Jackson divided the existing stage into two areas by using a second false proscenium painted to resemble the walls of a medieval castle framing an inner stage reached by three steps the width of the second proscenium. Apart from some photographs no records have survived of the production but it can be assumed that simple settings on the inner stage were changed behind traverse curtains while the performance continued uninterrupted in front. At the new theatre eighteen months later the permanent proscenium doors opened on to the apron stage, which then provided a third area for the actor to communicate intimately with the audience. When the young Peter Brook directed *King John* at the Rep in 1945 the designer Paul Shelving used the same formula (but without the apron which was abandoned in the 1930s): traverse curtains, a second proscenium painted like a stone castle and steps dividing an upper rostrum from the main stage.

In 1924, with a passing reference to Karl Immerman's Shakespeare productions in Düsseldorf as far back as 1840, Matthews stressed that the three-stage method was far from original.[23] Germany, as the reformers never tired of pointing out, had an impressive theatrical tradition which included small thriving regional theatres (a useful product of the formerly fragmented state) and a healthy but innovative respect for Shakespeare. The dominance of Meininger-style realism, however, meant experiments attempting to return Shakespeare to the flexibility of his original staging conditions had tended to produce a clash of conventions. The 'Shakespeare-stage' constructed at the Munich Residenztheater in 1889 by Jocza Savits and Kurt Lautenschläger resulted in productions where a series of detailed pictorial back-cloths, hung in the inner stage behind an elaborately-painted false proscenium, created a disjunction with the austerity of the bare middle and fore-stage. Although the basic model was abandoned in 1906, a second Shakespeare-stage in a simpler form was deployed by Eugen Kilian and Julius Klein again at the Residenztheater but inspired by the relief-stage of the newly-built Munich Künstlertheatre. The architect of the Künstler, Max Littman, built the theatre to the specifications of the director Georg Fuchs, who wished to initiate a festive collaboration in dance–drama between actor and spectator. The actors entered through permanent proscenium doors to perform primarily on the shallow broad fore-stage to an audience united in a single sweep of steeply-raked seating. A second adaptable proscenium divided the middle stage from the rear stage where perspective scenery could be set if necessary. Max Reinhardt, whose productions of Shakespeare in Berlin had achieved both fabulous decorative realism and continuity by the use of multiple built sets on the revolving stage of the Deutsches Theater, came to direct at the Künstler in the summer of 1909. The unaccustomed severity of the Künstler staging conditions compelled a radical simplification of Reinhardt's scenic assumptions which had a significant effect on his later work.[24]

The influence of German theatre — and Reinhardt's experiments in particular — on British innovation during this period of radical change is crucial. Poel not only saw Savits' Munich production of *King Lear* but met and corresponded with him. William Archer never tired of brandishing the example of German subsidised theatre to the British public, and subsequently saw and described Reinhardt's early Shakespeare productions. In 1909 Martin-Harvey brought Reinhardt's non-illusionist production of *The Taming of the Shrew* to London and in 1910 Barker met Reinhardt and visited theatres in Berlin and Düsseldorf.[25] Dennis Kennedy has pointed out that designs for Reinhardt's productions of *The Winter's Tale* by Emil Orlick in 1906, and a Craig-influenced *King Lear* in 1908 by

45

Carl Czeschka, anticipated Norman Wilkinson's decorations for Barker's Savoy Shakespeare. There is no evidence that Barry Jackson ever saw Reinhardt's work in pre-war Germany: more likely he benefited from what Kennedy calls the 'wireless messages' from Europe crackling with new ideas. In 1911, however, Basil Dean, at twenty-three the director of the newly-established Liverpool Repertory Theatre, travelled to Germany to return enthused by continental stagecraft and especially the lighting systems he had seen. At both the Deutsches and the Künstler a form of the Fortuny lighting system was in operation. In order to achieve the effect of natural direct and diffused sunlight Mariano Fortuny devised a technique, used in conjunction with a silk 'sky-dome', where pure white light was thrown on to bands of coloured silk that acted as reflectors which then diffused the light. In Germany the silk dome which deteriorated quickly was replaced by a plaster or concrete version. Not only did the system banish wrinkled back-cloths to produce a near-perfect illusion of sky but the possibilities for imaginative use in non-realistic drama appeared endless. Dean installed a system in Liverpool, and in 1912, gave a letter of introduction to the director of the Künstler to Sam Cooke, Barry Jackson's former colleague from Frank Osborn's office and the designated architect for the new Birmingham theatre.

As Cooke later explained, there was no example in Britain of the kind of building which Jackson envisaged. 'A small theatre, every seat-holder having an uninterrupted view of the stage, an intimate feeling between the audience and the players being the keynote of the design'.[26] In Manchester and Liverpool the new repertory companies had to be content with converted nineteenth-century theatres. When Cooke made his three-week tour of German theatres he must have been conscious that German architects led the world. Ultimately, despite the striking resemblance between the Birmingham Rep and the Künstler, none of the theatres he saw provided an exact model. Indeed, as Cooke later pointed out, the Germans would have built the new playhouse in a park while he had to settle for a site in Station Street and a frontage of 43 feet. The theatre which opened in February 1913 was a compromise — 'almost obscenely functional' as Bamber Gascoigne remarked fifty years later.[27] When the apron stage was removed, the proscenium framed an acting area which was virtually as deep as it was wide and perfectly suited to modern realistic prose drama. With the apron in place, together with the proscenium doors, the design looked back to the eighteenth-century Georgian theatre and acquired the intimacy and flexibility needed for poetic drama in general and Shakespeare in particular.

Chapter Four
Shakespeare in the New Theatre: 1913-1919

Perhaps the most significant factor about Rep Shakespeare in the first phase of the theatre's existence was the consistency of approach, even during the difficult years of the First World War. In the theatre outside Birmingham, traditional values and commercial pressures ensured that change was both gradual and desultory. Barker's production of *A Midsummer Night's Dream* at the Savoy in February 1914, with its semi-abstract forest curtains and golden fairies, seemed to represent the flamboyant justification for all the struggles of the previous decade. Despite the furious debate it provoked, the success of its ninety-nine performances should have opened the flood-gates to the Shakespeare revolution. But the war, declared on 4 August, halted inter-European cultural exchange and effectively ended Barker's practical work in the British theatre. Certainly no-one in 1914 who attended the small-scale traditional productions mounted spasmodically at the Old Vic (against the better judgment of its eccentric manager Lilian Baylis) could have guessed where that tentative venture would lead. During 1913 there had been other experiments. For *The Taming of the Shrew* staged at the Prince of Wales's Theatre, John Martin-Harvey brought together the influences of both Poel and Reinhardt, in a production which, despite a heavily-cut text, created a strong meta-theatrical quality. Seated on an apron stage with his back to the audience, Christopher Sly watched the taming story unfold through a succession of false prosceniums where costumed stage-hands moved scenic accessories.

In Manchester, however, eight months after the opening of Birmingham Rep, Lewis Casson directed *Julius Caesar* at the Gaiety

Theatre in an attempt 'to retain some of the splendours of Tree whilst at the same time incorporating some of the ideas of Poel'.[1] Hugh Fremantle's four basic sets combined with a temporary apron stage and decorative front curtains pleased the majority of the critics but audiences were poor, exacerbating deteriorating finances, and Miss Horniman was appalled by what she damned as 'a freakish production'. A row ensued and Casson resigned. In Birmingham there was no danger of a comparable clash and for Jackson there was no question of a return to 'the splendours of Tree'. The eleven Shakespearian plays which were staged between February 1913 and June 1918, when Drinkwater resigned his full-time work with the company, were all mounted according to the same comparatively austere formula. In April 1913 *Twelfth Night* reappeared, together with productions of *The Merry Wives of Windsor* and *King John*. In June *The Merchant of Venice* was performed for a week and in October *Henry IV Part One* was the first Shakespeare of the new season.

For the first few years each play usually ran for a week although there were occasional fortnight runs and a 'true repertory' fortnight of modern plays mounted in 1914. 'True repertory' it was argued, created audience resistance and placed a heavy burden on stage-management staff, especially as storage space was restricted. In March 1914 a new building in Hinckley Street provided store rooms, a carpenter's workshop and a scene-painting room. Some stock scenery accumulated, but the theatre prided itself on producing freshly designed and constructed sets as often as possible. Indeed as thirty-four new productions had been staged by the end of 1913 it looks as though the company was eager to wring every ounce of opportunity out of their new-found resources. The weekly routine of performance, rehearsal, planning and construction must have been exhausting and many a first-night audience had to be content with the uncertain standards of a dress rehearsal. John Drinkwater recalled spending twenty minutes prompting Margaret Chatwin 'in acute discomfort within the confines of an oak settle upon which she sat through a scene taking from me what she could of the true text of a Merry Wife of Windsor'.[2] But in 1924, while acknowledging the lack of finished excellence, Matthews defended the system. It was, he claimed, much easier to mount a production quickly with a group of

49

people who knew each other well and what was lost in polish was gained in spontaneity and freshness.

A repertoire of Shakespeare was built up which permitted a short festival each April — a tradition which began in 1911 when the Pilgrims staged all three of their previous productions. For the tercentenary of Shakespeare's death in 1916, five plays were performed between 22 April and 6 May. Again *Twelfth Night* was revived, directed by Drinkwater with new designs by Jackson. *The Merchant of Venice, The Tempest* and *The Merry Wives of Windsor* were also revivals. The new play, *Macbeth*, directed by Drinkwater with Harcourt Williams in the title role, had its first performance on 29 April and 15 May saw the beginning of a week's run of Harcourt Williams' production of *As You Like It*, which he first directed at the Rep in February 1914.

As a rule plays were cast from within the company although occasionally guest actors were engaged for special parts. In October 1913 additional actors, both professional and amateur, were brought in to supply the large cast needed for Arnold Pinchard's production of *Henry IV Part One* — which may have been the reason why it ran for a fortnight. The experienced Shakespearian Allan Wilkie was invited to play Falstaff but some criticism suggested that he was acting in a different, older tradition to the rest of the company. There were complaints that he was excessively padded and that his voice was too loud for the small auditorium. When Osmund Willson played the role in both parts of *Henry IV* and *Merry Wives* in 1920 and 1921, he was a full member of the company. Although Willson lacked the traditional physique, E. A. Baughan thought him one of the best Falstaffs he had seen. Baughan's comments in the *Daily News* on 29 November 1920 are an indication of all that was gained from the theatre's approach to Shakespeare:

> He indulged in none of the exaggerated business which usually spoils the part and his playing was full of unforced humour. For once in my experience Falstaff was allowed to have his true importance as a kind of chorus. He acted as a foil to the historical heroics of the play and as humorous commentary on them, which is surely what Shakespeare intended.

Naturally even a sympathetic audience such as the Rep enjoyed would hope to see their favourite Shakespearian characters brought to life by actors capable of exploiting each opportunity to the full. The romantic heroines posed a particular problem. As we have seen, Cecily Byrne failed to satisfy all her critics with her Viola in 1913. It was the same when she played Rosalind in *As You Like It* in 1914. The *Birmingham Daily Post* of 9 February recorded that she gave an intelligent but undistinguished reading of the part. In 1915 the same newspaper complained of her performance in *The Tempest* that she 'reduced Miranda to a domesticated young lady with little imagination' (19 April 1915). Mielle Maund who took over Miranda and Viola in 1916 proved no better. On 24 April the *Post* commented that 'as Miranda she was resolutely pleased at everything and nothing . . . When Prospero told the story of his banishment she declared with cheerful emphasis that "her heart bleeds" for the sorrow she had brought upon him but she smiled as gaily as if he had made a joke she did not quite understand'. As Viola she was 'far too busy with little tricks and anxious artifice and finesse. Viola watching Orsino with the hidden fervour and intensity of love willing to be his envoy of courtship or to die at his hand, needs other methods' (13 May 1916). In all fairness, however, it must be admitted that prettiness and good-natured competence were often all that was expected and relatively few hoped for more. *The Stage* of 12 February 1914 described Cecily Byrne's Rosalind as 'a perfect golden heroine'.

One highly successful importation into the company for the Shakespeare season of April 1916 was Phyllis Relph, who had substituted for Lillah McCarthy as Viola and Helena in the Savoy *Twelfth Night* and *A Midsummer Night's Dream*. Earlier she had played Margaret in Shaw's first commercial success *Fanny's First Play*: just one of several actors from the McCarthy/Barker-managed production who would offer much to the Rep in years to come. In Birmingham she was praised for her Portia in an undistinguished revival of *The Merchant of Venice*. Of the revival of *As You Like It* the *Post* critic wrote:

> She did not vulgarise Rosalind into the romping hoyden of some actresses: beneath the high spirited and witty boyishness of Ganymede she preserved always the grace and womanliness of Rosalind . . . incomparably above any other performances of the

Shakespearean women boys who have been seen in Birmingham for many years. She sometimes laughs her speeches into incoherence; perhaps to mask an occasional uncertainty of memory, but otherwise her Rosalind is almost without fault . . . at once human and romantic (*Birmingham Daily Post*, 16 April 1916)

In December 1919 the distinguished Bensonian Dorothy Green, who would become a leading figure in William Bridges-Adams' New Shakespeare Company at Stratford, played Rosalind. For Crompton Rhodes she presented a 'live, mercurial, understanding, passionate woman, passing without violence from one gradation of feeling to another' (*Birmingham Daily Post*, 2 December 1919).

That Margaret Chatwin was an impressive tragic actress is apparent from reviews of her Constance in 1913 and Lady Macbeth in 1916. She also seems to have been a successful Isabella in the 1918 *Measure for Measure*. John Drinkwater wrote in 1923 of her ability in roles that required: 'immense emotional staying power . . . Margaret Chatwin I have always considered to have a greater purely tragic power than any other English actress of my generation. Her intellectual control did not perhaps quite match her superb rhythmic sense of poetry and character, otherwise she would have been, as Broadway has it, a world beater'.[3] As Beatrice in 1919 and Katharine in *The Taming of the Shrew* in 1918 she was given credit for playing what was considered against her natural physical type. As Portia she was never really satisfactory. After her appearance in the final revival of *The Merchant of Venice* in 1919, the *Post* critic commented 'Mr Jackson would be doing a great service if he would discover a young actress to play these sweet heroines of fantasy, but she needs to be a Vesta Tilley on the plane of poetry' (*Birmingham Daily Post*, 26 May 1919). The arrival of Gwen Ffrangçon-Davies in 1921 provided an actress who was physically slight but with sufficient maturity and emotional stamina. With all the lyric qualities required for a romantic heroine, she proved to be an ideal Juliet.

After the fashion of their Pilgrim days, Barry Jackson and John Drinkwater continued to act themselves. Drinkwater (as John Darnley) played Sir Richard Vernon in *Henry IV Part One* in 1913, and in 1914 was commended for his Jaques in *As You Like It* 'an effective middle way between rhetoric and melodramatic bitterness'

(*Birmingham Daily Post*, 9 February 1914). He continued to play Malvolio for the second and third revivals of *Twelfth Night* until he took over the direction of 1916. But he seems to have lacked the sureness of touch as an actor which he increasingly acquired as a director. In 1916 in his own production of *The Merry Wives of Windsor* he played Nym with Scott Sunderland's Bardolph and Harcourt Williams' Pistol. It seems the trio added excessive rumbustiousness to what was otherwise a well-balanced production. In 1918 the *Era* (1 May) described him as a 'heavy' Angelo in his own production of *Measure for Measure*.

As a tall well-built man, Jackson had a commanding stage presence and a fine voice. He was praised for his performance of the Bastard in *King John* as well as Hotspur in *Henry IV Part One* in 1913. He played Duke Frederick and spoke the words of Hymen in a revival of *As You Like It* in 1914. One of his last Shakespearian roles was the Prologue in the 1922 *Romeo and Juliet*. In *Discovery* Drinkwater compared Jackson the designer to Jackson the actor:

> He had a roving eye. To be on stage with him was to be distracted by the knowledge that he was inspecting Mrs . . .'s opera cloak in the fourth row of the stalls, or speculating on the possible use of the backcloth for the production after next. He and I played many parts together, and it was unusual for him to give or take a cue precisely.[4]

Looking back on her years with the company during the early twenties, Gwen Ffrangçon-Davies considered that the supporting casts were rarely much more than adequate. She suggested that Pilgrim stalwarts like Isabel Thornton who played the Nurse to her Juliet in 1922 were little more than 'gifted amateurs'. For her, Barry Jackson was too loyal to the provincial actors who had supported him in the past.[5] His friend and companion Scott Sunderland continued to act with the company for more than thirty years (his last Shakespearian role at the Rep was as an implacable Pandulph in Peter Brook's *King John*) but he was not naturally a subtle actor unless given careful direction. His Orlando in 1914 and 1916 was described at best as 'manly' and at worst as merely 'noisy'. He was most successful in roles which required a robust approach. John Gielgud wrote in *An Actor and his Time* that Sunderland played

'Mercutio in a very violent style. He used to knock me about on the stage which made me nervous and threw me off balance'. However Gielgud goes on to say of Jackson, who gave him the opportunity to play Romeo, his first important role, in 1924 'He was not certain that he wanted stars in his company; he believed in a repertory company — which is why I got the part of Romeo'.[6] Just so: other young actors of promise would follow on and benefit in their turn — although Gielgud himself, Ellen Terry's great-nephew and imbued with the family tradition of star acting, would doubtless have found fame anyway. But there is more than a hint in this statement that 'a repertory company' implied a less than perfect standard of acting. As the company gathered strength and reputation it could offer protection as a place to grow, where talent could be nurtured and survive the occasional failure. On arrival at the Rep in 1921 after years of miserable touring in musical comedy, Gwen Ffrangçon-Davies was agreeably surprised by the courteous and scholarly Bache Matthews, who as an unlikely theatrical business manager, typified the Rep's serious, committed ambience. What was even more agreeable was the year's contract on £6 a week which included a month's holiday on full pay.

In the early years especially Jackson appears to have been more interested in plays than players and in inexperienced actors and directors of promise rather than stars. In the Rep productions of Shakespeare, even when the acting was faulty, the plays were the focus of attention and the reviews always acknowledged this. The choice of plays does seem to have reflected the strengths of the company approach. Whether because contemporary taste preferred Shakespearian comedy or because plays which required a commanding central performance were considered unsuitable, the great tragedies were not a regular part of the repertoire. *Macbeth* in 1916 called on Harcourt Williams who had both acted and directed at the Rep in 1914. But by then he was an actor of considerable experience — and yet another graduate of *Fanny's First Play* in which he played Count O'Dowda. Even so the reviews were ambivalent about his performance and *Macbeth* was not revived with another actor. When E. Stuart Vinden played Othello in 1920, the casting deliberately flouted traditional notions about the voice and physique of the character. Just how controversial the choice was can be borne out by the fact that Vinden played Ariel in the 1915 and 1916 productions of *The Tempest*: the first man to do so since the seventeenth century. A plan to stage the First Quarto of *Hamlet* with Vinden in the leading role had to be abandoned when illness forced a temporary retirement from the theatre in 1921. When *Hamlet* was finally produced in 1925, an entirely new approach to the play allowed for another unconventional choice for the central character.

At first the selection of plays appears resolutely traditional: *Twelfth Night*, *The Merry Wives of Windsor*, *The Merchant of Venice* and *As You Like It* were the most frequently performed. By 1922 *Twelfth Night* had reappeared eight times with three directors and at least three new designs. Of course, the theatre's approach was far from traditional and whereas the commercial theatre could seldom risk unfamiliar plays such as *The Two Gentlemen of Verona*, *Measure for Measure* or *Love's Labour's Lost*, the Rep could and did mount these plays, confident that the lack of glamorous starring parts was of no consequence. *The Two Gentlemen of Verona* was staged twice: in 1917 and then again in 1924. On neither occasion was it a great success. The 1917 production was badly under-rehearsed, but audiences seem to have appreciated its rarity value. *Measure for Measure* in 1918, however, earned the judgement from the *Birmingham Daily Post* on 24 April that 'this tragi-comedy is one of the greatest of Shakespeare's plays'. Apart from Poel's Manchester/Stratford production there had been only one major revival of the play, with Oscar Asche and Lily Brayton at the Adelphi Theatre in 1906, since the beginning of the century. Crompton Rhodes in the *Post*, discussing its neglect in the theatre, acknowledged the hypocrisy of a society which damned the play's treatment of sexuality and then enjoyed the same theme, suitably disguised, in most modern farce. He went on to say 'The Repertory Theatre ideals of simplicity and directness are peculiarly suitable for *Measure for Measure*: since no elaboration is allowed to pervert the presentation and nothing extraneous is allowed to impose upon the purpose'.

In late 1919 *Love's Labour's Lost*, directed and designed by Jackson, proved to be a most successful venture. Jackson devised a permanent setting of three arched entrances set in the walls of a courtyard in a formal garden. Behind were the simple shapes of trees and a miniature vista of the park and Navarre's palace. In the centre of the stage was a pedestalled cupid which Stuart Vinden as Berowne leaped on as he persuaded his friends to give way to the power of love. The *Birmingham Gazette* (24 November 1919) pointed out that 'it is a play of groups rather than of individual protagonists' which was ideally suited to the company on top form who allowed the play 'to develop into a jolly romp suited to the lavish experimentalism of the young author'. The production played initially for one week from 22 to 28 November, but proved so popular that it was immediately revived for another week on 15 December. Then in 1920 it was revived again from 23 April to 4 May when it was seen by no less than William Archer who rudely judged the play and its 'archaic puerilities . . . to be a standing admonition to dramatic critics to be gentle in their judgement of a first play' (*Illustrated Sporting and Dramatic News*, 15 May 1920). But the play remained a favourite of Jackson's. Twenty six years later he gave it to Peter Brook for his directorial debut at the Shakespeare Memorial Theatre.

In 1921 R. Crompton Rhodes wrote that 'Mr Barry Jackson has had a greater experience of producing Shakespeare in full text than any other man in the world'. This extraordinary statement was made in an article entitled 'The Full Text Controversy' published in his newspaper on 16 April. Rhodes interviewed Jackson and William Bridges-Adams, the man Ben Greet dubbed 'Unabridges-Adams' after his first season as director of the New Shakespeare Company at the Shakespeare Memorial Theatre in 1919. From late 1914 until 1917 Greet had himself been responsible for the direction of seventeen plays for the newly established Shakespeare Company at the Old Vic. Limited resources and cramped, ramshackle conditions however, ensured that the amiable Greet directed according to his well-tried formula of stock business and heavily-cut texts.

Bridges-Adams saw his initial no-cuts policy as 'experiments for I wanted to find out really what the plays were made of themselves when left alone'. By 1921 he had modified his views:

A great play is not a fragile thing like a sonnet; it achieves itself only through actors and spectators. I doubt whether either of these can hurt it so much through incompetence or ignorance as those brilliant enemies of the theatre who prefer still-life perfection to live

perfection. For all his enormities it was Tree who kept Shakespeare
alive in our generation, not the highbrows
(*Birmingham Daily Post*, 16 April 1921)

Eventually, as Sally Beauman has pointed out, Bridges-Adams cut
Shakespeare's plays very thoroughly indeed, 'occasionally savaging
them in a manner reminiscent of Benson and Victorian actor
managers at their worst'.[7]

Experience of viable professional production does not appear to
have altered the Rep's policy. Up until 1919 the majority of
Shakespeare was directed by Drinkwater, but the approach to each
production was so much a corporate effort that it is difficult to know
who made the textual decisions. Much later in his life, Jackson
himself prepared texts even when he left full responsibility for other
aspects of production to his directors.

What Rhodes's article terms textual 'excrescences' were sometimes
removed. *The Merry Wives of Windsor* is an obvious example. It had
always been a popular play with Birmingham audiences, a regular
Benson piece, and the Rep productions seem to have improved
steadily with each of the five revivals. What was considered tedious
or obscure was removed including Parson Evans' Latin lesson and
all the references to the horse-stealing plot. The 1916 prompt-book
shows a loss of about 145 lines whereas when A. E. Filmer directed
the play in 1920 only about 128 lines were cut. In the 1916 *Macbeth*
all the Hecate sequences were omitted but, unusually, the whole of
the long debate between Malcolm and Macduff in IV.iii remained,
although the talk with the English doctor about the 'Evil' cured by
the King went. Occasionally the policy rebounded on the director's
head as audiences became more sensitive to textual loss. In 1920
when Filmer removed the important debate between Emilia and
Desdemona about the consequences of adultery — 'a great price for
a small vice' — in IV.iii of *Othello* there were several protests. In
1915 and 1916, the omission of Prospero's Epilogue to *The Tempest*
on the dubious grounds that it was unShakespearian provoked
adverse comment as did the loss of Ferdinand and Miranda's chess
game. It was an otherwise interesting production. Not only was
there a male Ariel (prompted, some claimed, by Granville Barker's
Savoy Puck), but Jackson created a blue and purple northern island

57

where a grey Ariel and blue Caliban (Ion Swinley) reflected the landscape, and the red costumes of the shipwrecked court created a startling contrast. Felix Aylmer's Prospero, made up to resemble Plato, inhabited a cell carved out of the rock like a blue-stone classical temple. In the face of the radical design which rejected the usual lush tropicana, the loss of the Epilogue and the substitution of extra stage business seems to represent an almost Tree-like approach on Drinkwater's part. As Prospero concluded the play proper with an invitation to Alonso and the other courtiers to enter his cave, music began to play. Stephano and Trinculo re-emerged with trenchers and cups and sat eating with the Boatswain and the Ship's Master, in a circle round a table. Caliban climbed from under the back of the table and sat eating an apple while Ariel gathered up Prospero's cloak and staff and threw them over the back of the rocks which took up the greater part of the stage. As the curtain fell still with music playing, Ariel leaped off to freedom.

In general, however, the texts remained dominant. In the 1919 *Much Ado about Nothing*, directed by Conal O'Riordan, a mere fifteen lines were lost. When the two parts of *Henry IV* were staged, *Part One* in November 1920 and *Part Two* in April 1921, it might be expected that more would be cut, especially as in 1921 both parts were performed on the afternoon and evening of Shakespeare's birthday. In *Part One* about 275 lines went including some of the very lengthy speeches of the King to Prince Hal in II.i and the whole of the parley between Sir Walter Blunt and the rebels before the battle of Shrewsbury. However in *Part Two*, which is the longer play, only fifty-five lines are cut from the prompt-text.

Both Jackson and Bridges-Adams agreed that 'offensive' passages ought to be excised. What Sally Beauman has described as a 'delicate squeamishness'[8] in Bridges-Adams' temperament was to some extent shared by Barry Jackson. Tom English, Jackson's Press Officer and then secretary for many years, recalled that as late as 1946 Jackson wanted Paul Scofield to cut out Lucio's slander of the Duke in *Measure for Measure* 'But it is certain that when he makes water his urine is congeal'd ice'. Scofield refused.[9] It must be acknowledged, however, that sensitivity to explicit references to sexual organs or basic bodily functions was common in the period. Barker believed in a degree of discreet expurgation, while William

Archer who had championed Ibsen's more oblique treatment of sexual issues, was, as he put it in a discussion of the Rep's 1920 *Othello*, 'irreconcilably opposed' to 'all the Elizabethan crudities of speech'. Shakespeare's 'disagreeable archaisms' were not appropriate in civilised modern production (*Illustrated Sporting and Dramatic News*, 15 May 1920). In the Rep's early productions any obvious 'crudities' such as Shylock's observation that 'others, when the bagpipe sings i' the' nose/Cannot contain their urine', were removed. In *Love's Labour's Lost* the reference to Jaquenetta's pregnancy was omitted, making Don Armado's penance seem a little excessive. A more serious loss was from Falstaff's opening discussion with his page in I.ii of *Henry IV Part Two*: an exchange which virtually encapsulates the profoundly-altered comic tone of the play:

> *Falstaff*   Sirrah, you giant, what says the doctor to my water?
>
> *Page*   He said sir, the water itself was a good healthy water; but for the party that owed it, he might have moe diseases then he knew for (lines 1–4)

But there was no wholesale bowdlerisation and in this respect *Measure for Measure* was a significant challenge to the director's nerve. It is interesting that the 1918 prompt-book reveals increasingly bold decisions to preserve as much of the text as was decently possible. Ultimately about 105 lines were cut but it appears that an initial plan to chop a further twenty-three lines was reconsidered. As might be expected a good deal of Lucio's scurrilous remarks went as well as the more blatant references to Mistress Overdone's profession and the joke about Pompey's bum. The story of Froth and Mistress Elbow's longing for prunes was modified. The majority of the reinstated lines refer to Juliet's pregnancy. It was decided that Mistress Overdone must explain Claudio's crime. 'It is for getting Madam Julietta with child'. Also the exchange between Claudio and Lucio in the same scene was retained:

> *Lucio*   What is't murder?
> *Claudio*   No.
> *Lucio*   Lechery?
> *Claudio*   Call it so. (II.i. 130–33)

The news in II.ii. 16 that Juliet is 'very near her hour', was reconsidered as was the Duke's question to Juliet in II.ii 'So then, it seems, your most offenceful act/Was mutually committed'. In III.ii as Isabella explains her predicament to Claudio, her words at line 103 'That I should do what I abhor to name' and at 140 'Is't not a kind of incest' and 151 'Mercy to thee would prove itself a bawd' were all reinstated. The two long debates between Isabella and Angelo in II.ii and iv were given virtually in full. Only the most explicit demands in II.iv to Isabella to lay down her body were removed. The Duke's plan for Isabella and Mariana to change places was made quite clear as were the final revelations in V.i, although the frankest statements concerning sexual 'knowledge' were lost. At the very end however, the director shrank from Lucio's marriage to a 'punk'. Marriage itself was deemed sufficient punishment.

One great blessing of the policy was that there was no scene transposition — that great aid to the Edwardian scene shifters. The original narrative sequence of the plays was preserved. The gifts the theatre in Birmingham gave its audiences were not only unfamiliar plays in fuller texts but also minor characters perhaps not seen on the English stage in living memory. The clown and the herald included in the 1920 *Othello* are even now comparatively rare. In *Romeo and Juliet* the folk who people the household of the Capulets were allowed to stay: the cooks and serving men, Anthony and Potpan, and the musicians, Simon Catling, Hugh Rebeck and James Soundpost.

It would be an exaggeration to claim that the cameo role of the Duke of Arragon in *The Merchant of Venice* was never seen on the Victorian and Edwardian stage but productions which included the character were exceptional. At the Rep W. Ribton Haines played the part in 1913 and again in 1915 when *The Stage* singled him out as a 'comic aristocratic noodle' (21 October 1915) and the *Post* liked his 'air of amiability, complacency and assurance' (15 October 1915). The play itself was very familiar. It was a constant feature of Benson's repertoire and Tree included it in each of his Shakespeare Festivals from 1908 to 1913. A succession of leading actors had played Shylock. With Hamlet and Richard III, it was one of the great testing roles by which an actor established his reputation and frequently signalled a revolutionary change in acting styles. Henry Irving of course, was the Shylock of his generation, turning the character into a tragic figure. Although the myth that Irving invariably cut the final act has been dispelled by Alan Hughes,[10] the tradition of using the play as a vehicle for the leading actor's Shylock inevitably distorted the romantic comedy. The story of Portia and Bassanio was heavily trimmed, relegated to the position of subplot and frequently trivialised. In 1898 William Poel attempted to redress the balance by playing Shylock as a grotesque in a red wig. In relentlessly depriving the character of both pathos and dignity, Poel's version was as extreme as Irving's.

The number of revivals of the play at the Rep was exceeded only by *Twelfth Night* and *The Merry Wives of Windsor*. It was first produced on 7 June 1913 and there were three revivals directed by John Drinkwater. Finally Jackson (who played Bassanio in 1915) directed a specially-requested schools' matinée on 24 May 1919 where he also played the Prince of Morocco. It is obvious that Drinkwater's production tried to present the play as a romantic comedy. The critic of the *Birmingham Mail* on 18 October 1915, described it as 'a play about happy people which should commence in sunshine and end in music, love and laughter'. The text was cut but with little concession to accepted practice for the play was staged in approximately two and three-quarter hours with two short intervals: the first after II.vi and the second after III.iv. The characters Salanio, Salerio and Salarino were conflated so that only Salanio and Salarino appeared. Portia's servants Balthazar and Stephano were combined into one: Balthazar in 1913, Stephano for all the other revivals. These small speaking parts created problems for a company stretched to its limits by the larger casts required for Shakespeare. It seems to have been normal practice to bring in local amateur actors to provide a few supernumeraries. For *The Merchant* there were four magnificoes for the trial scene and four ladies to attend Portia. Typically a few lines were lost in V.i concerning who would or would not sleep with Portia and Nerissa which meant that the play ended with Portia promising to 'answer all things faithfully', rather than an anticipation of the joys of 'couching with the doctor's clerk'. The whole of the conversation between Launcelot, Jessica and Lorenzo in III.v was omitted. The scene interrupts the transition to Antonio's trial and raises awkward questions about Jessica's ambiguous position in the narrative. As the second interval was placed after the preceding scene where Portia reveals her scheme to rescue Antonio, the production's third act began with the trial.

In contrast to Jackson's early memories of Irving's version, there was no superfluous music. In 1913 the music for 'Tell me where is fancy bred' was composed by Arnold Pinchard's son Lester and was sung in the wings by a group of women accompanied by a spinet. The play began with celesta bells and a short flourish from a cornet and drum. Subsequently the cornet and drum heralded the entrances of Morocco and Arragon and the Duke of Venice. After creating the carnival atmosphere in Venice, the celesta bells introduced Bassanio to Belmont and finally provded the 'sweet music' for Lorenzo and Jessica in V.i. A combined flourish ended the play. To bolster dwindling audiences immediately after the outbreak of the First World War, a small orchestra consisting of a string quartet and a piano was introduced and for *The Merchant of Venice* played sixteenth and seventeenth-century music. For the tercentenary celebrations in 1916 Arnold Dolmetsch, whose music for Poel's productions had so delighted Shaw, came with his family to give a recital of early settings of Shakespeare's songs.

As always, immediacy of effect and continuity of action was achieved by the use of three acting areas and alternating curtains. The first scene was played before the tableau curtains on the apron stage with Antonio, Salarino and Salanio entering from the apron doors. The main features of the permanent setting were two marble pillars which formed the second inner proscenium on the central stage. A grey curtain drawn between the pillars created an interior for the second scene in Belmont where Portia and Nerissa shared a bowl of sweets while they discussed Portia's suitors. The full setting was revealed for the third scene and the introduction to Shylock. No photograph of the set has survived but reviews of the revival in October 1915 described how the two pillars gave the effect of limitless sky. Two semi-circular steps led up to the inner raised stage where a balustrade and the blue sky provided by the cyclorama suggested the Venetian city of canals. In 1955 Jackson recalled:

some attempt to recapture the opalescent tones of the lagoons and palaces as I had seen them in the bright light of the early spring. The result was obtained by using material of any colour with a glossy surface covered with multi-coloured fine net, the two together regardless of shade giving a milky appearance of the watery city.[11]

The trial scene used a scarlet and gold hanging — possibly one of the Carpaccio tapestry curtains — set against a reddened cyclorama. The Duke and four magnificoes sat in a semi-circle on the upper stage with a clerk seated below. Shylock entered through the left proscenium door and stood left above Gratiano and Salario, remaining in this position, moving only slightly, throughout the entire scene. Portia and Nerissa also made their entrances from the left: Nerissa went to stand right of the Duke while Portia remained stage left of him. In 1915 there were comments on the striking effect of Portia's yellow and white robes which contrasted with Antonio's gold-coloured costume as he stood on the opposite side of the stage. Bache Matthews wrote that the costumes were inspired by the same fifteenth-century source used for the Pilgrim production of *The Two Gentlemen of Verona*, but instead of very bright colours, delicate pastel shades were achieved by specially-dyed fabrics. The critic of the *Birmingham Daily Post* (18 October 1915) was delighted by this 'fantaisie in pastel . . . in the colours of Watteau and Fragonard — amber, honeyed yellow, and tarnished gold, turquoise blue, fresh and faded pink'. After IV.ii was played on the apron, the tableau curtains were raised to discover Jessica and Lorenzo in the moonlight at Belmont. The cyclorama was transformed into a deep blue Italian night sky spangled with stars which made a beautiful setting for the final sequence of the play and earned praise through all the revivals.

The production in June 1913 attracted little attention. It came at the end of a succession of Shakespeare productions; hard work was taking its toll, and the few reviews agree that despite an innovative approach to the play, much improvement was needed. Aylmer played Bassanio, Frank Moore, Antonio, while Jackson took Morocco. Margaret Chatwin as Portia began well but her effectiveness crumbled in the final act as her memory failed. Ironically the one performance which stood out as exceptional was

Ivor Barnard's Shylock. *The Stage* (13 June 1913) noted that 'Ivor Barnard acted the part with much vigour and intensity and in many ways gave a reading differing from that of the dignified noble Jew which Sir Henry Irving's acting made the popular version'.

Barnard had trained in Benson's school and after touring with various Shakespeare companies had spent 1912 playing Flawner Bannel in *Fanny's First Play*. He joined the Rep company at Drinkwater's invitation to play Fabian in the first *Twelfth Night* and was subsequently praised for his Parson Evans in *The Merry Wives of Windsor* in April 1913. He was a small man and his dry humour made him a successful Touchstone in 1914. By 1915 when he came to play Shylock again, he was well known not only as a comic actor but as an impersonator of old men. The *Birmingham Daily Post* review praised Drinkwater's production 'in many ways the most individual, most sustained and most harmonious of the revivals'. It depended, the critic suggested, upon a new conception of Shylock. Ivor Barnard's portrayal was neither a caricature nor the 'strange romantic solitary figure' created by Irving. For the *Birmingham Mail*, the production's 'great merit' lay in its restoring to the play 'that proper balance which in the last half century the pride of the actor–manager has tended to upset'. The *Post* review went on to describe Barnard's performance:

> his Shylock is divested entirely of comedy — even that easiest of points, the magnificent Hebraism 'a wilderness of monkeys' was spoken with quiet sorrowful unstressed sincerity. In its subdued intensity it was a masterpiece of resource — every delicate inflection had subtlety, force and precision, every variation of pace responded to the inward thought.

It was noticed that Barnard never actually took centre-stage. In Tree's extravagantly physical performance as Shylock he had raged round the empty rooms of the home abandoned by Jessica, writhed on the ground in a paroxysm of rage and grief, and at the final sentence of enforced conversion, fainted into Tubal's arms. Barnard was impressive in stillness — moving only when necessary.

Several reviews in 1913 and 1915 commented on a refreshing lack of traditional stage business. Indeed the absence of much in the way of interpolated stage directions in the simple prompt-book which may have served from 1913 until 1919, suggests a rather static production. The *Birmingham Mail* on 18 October 1915 found it at times 'rather pale and montonous'. But the *Birmingham Daily Post* observed:

> The playing was subdued. Only the speaker of the moment was allowed a little rare gesture. When they were not acting the players stood in silence and immobility fading away into the decorations like a painted figure in low relief. This formal and finite arrangement had an unobtrusive quaintness as if Mr Drinkwater had discerned the enchanting possibilities of the group figures in the paste board theatre of childhood . . . the method of presentation recalls the faraway strivings of Lugne-Poe and W. B. Yeats and the old demands for the grace of figures in a dream and the fall of pure and low voices.

As Drinkwater broke away from traditional production values, he may have been remembering Yeats's demand for 'sustained external immobility' in heightened poetic performance despite the risk of alienating sections of his audience. During his association with Jackson's company, Drinkwater's work as a poet also extended like Yeats's into attempts to revive the art of verse drama: a perennial and for the most part, doomed preoccupation amongst would-be contemporary dramatists. During the war years, while the Georgian poets briefly flourished until the rigours of modernism pushed them into obscurity, five verse plays by Drinkwater were premièred at the Rep: *Rebellion* (1914), *The Storm* (1915), *The God of Quiet* (1916) *X=O, A Night of the Trojan War* and *Cophetua* (1917). That each was deeply committed, passionately spoken and staged with Jackson's simple evocative sets, did not make them enduringly effective theatre.

The first revival of *The Merchant of Venice* in 1915 was obviously the high point of Drinkwater's exploration of the play. The production was staged again on 1 December 1915 with an unchanged cast for four performances, but hoarseness handicapped Barnard's performance. The revival in May 1916 was described by the *Post* (4 May 1916) as a 'feeble travesty of former excellence'. This time Stuart Vinden played Shylock as 'no more than a Welsh lay-preacher annoyed at the conduct of a village debating society and mildly dejected at being outvoted.' Aylmer was an 'ordinary

Lorenzo', while Harcourt Williams played Gratiano with a good deal of superfluous stage business which the *Post* observed would have 'imperilled the harmony of the last presentation', but now seems to have provided much needed relief. Only Phyllis Relph's Portia won unqualified praise. The *Post* stated 'few Portias have counterfeited the boyishness, the young manliness of the learned Doctor of Laws so cleverly; the forensic delivery was indicated lightly and clearly'.

Vinden's wife Maud Gill played Jessica in 1916. She had been in the company since the second season, and not only acted but, because the war effort claimed many of the Rep's male staff, became stage manager — a position then unusual for a woman. Her memoirs, published in 1938, give a valuable insight into the back-stage dramas of noisy recalcitrant equipment, temperamental technicians, inept stage hands, forgetful actors and the sheer hard work and resourcefulness needed to sustain the Rep's programme. The fountain which played during the last act of *The Merchant* was a nightmare. For the production in 1913 T. Foden Flint, the Rep's first stage-manager, lay under the stage on his back blowing water up through a piece of iron tubing for fifteen minutes at every performance. In 1916 on the occasions when the stage-hands mastered the syphon Maud Gill, acting with Aylmer, had to combat the noise of plops and gurgles, and on one night the water began to flood the stage. At the same performance Aylmer's dagger caught in the grass matting which covered the 'bank' to reveal the indispensible collection of ginger-beer boxes which formed its foundation. In her account of the complex property lists required for modern detailed naturalistic drama, Gill adds: 'If a Shakespearian play were down for production we went about with peaceful hearts and happy faces. If we collected a few odd swords, a stool or two and some wooden goblets our troubles were practically at an end'[12] — a far cry from the demands of old-style Shakespeare.

However the effects were achieved, Jackson's work as a designer, devoted almost exclusively to classic or modern poetic drama, became increasingly successful. In 1955, rather dismissively, he stated that he had never heard any comments from the audience on his design experiments. But there is plenty of discussion in the reviews. Certainly commentators were alert to the possible influence of 'Barkerism' and the differences between what the *Birmingham Mail* review of the 1914 *As You Like It* dubbed as Jackson's 'penny plain' approach and the Barker/Wilkinson 'tuppence coloured' designs at the Savoy. Despite a preference for the Rep's simplicity the review warns against the potential for 'freakishness':

> On Saturday night we were presented with a background depicting a wall, painted with all the newness and realism of a child's conception of a straight wall, flanked by two wings bearing brown streaks on a green ground, or green streaks on a brown ground, and told this was the 'Orchard of Oliver's House' (9 February 1914).

The review in the *Stage* of the same production also included a troubled appraisal of Barker's methods in the Savoy *Dream* and objected both to the breaking down of the stage illusion of the fairies' 'fabled existence' as the actors crossed the proscenium barrier and the defiant display of the artifice of theatre. The writer's conclusion was that despite the unloading of massive stage-carpentry, 'it is still the picture, not the play that is the thing'. However, he went on to approve Jackson's Forest of Arden: 'it consisted mainly of several rows of brown shadowless tree trunks reaching up apparently to an illimitable height with the glow of a sunrise or moonlight shining through them. It was a conventionalised forest with conventionalised trees, but it did convey some sense of the depths of the wood' (12 February 1914). By 1916 when war-time theatre was dominated by the demand for high-gloss entertainment rather than the avant-garde, the *Stage* was citing the Rep as one of the few playhouses in the country where enterprising Shakespeare production could be found and went on to describe Jackson's design for *Twelfth Night* which enabled the play to be staged in little more than two and a half hours:

> The principal scene resembles the loggia of an Italian villa, and is designed to represent the atmosphere of the whole comedy. There is a plain background of a deep blue sky. Against this rises a terrace with decorative orange trees and four cream-coloured columns with black pedestals and tops. Two shallow steps extending right across the stage lead to a lower platform at each end of which stands a square pillar with similar black terminals; a short flight of semi-circular steps leads down to the stage proper and the apron stage exterior (16 March 1916).

67

All the scenes in Olivia's household were lit with a warm amber light.

A similar approach was adopted for *Much Ado About Nothing* which Jackson along with Guy Kortright designed in 1919. Jackson described the set in 1955: 'Again a solid loggia was built. The centre was arched over a flight of some dozen steps; on either side of the arch were two square openings with balustrades, and beneath these two square blocks on the stage itself'.[13] The columns were painted to represent white marble and the floor was a pavement of black and white squares. In 1921, in a talk to the Birmingham Art Circle, Jackson explained that he had originally seen the play in the Renaissance world of Veronese. He envisaged 'stiff whale-boned dresses and ruffs, great colonnades and terraces and heavy curtains falling in gigantic folds'. His director this time was Conal O'Riordan (who had worked with the Irish Players), who saw something hard and crystalline in the humour and wanted a sharp, clearly defined design. Kortright and Jackson took their cue from the Sicilian wars of the King of Arragon and turned to the early fourteenth century 'to find a certain angularity' in the costumes of the period. The men wore tunics with square fitting belts worn low over the thighs, long hanging false sleeves and high collars. The women wore stiff square tabards down the front and back of their dresses and their hair was confined in tightly-bound wimples. In a production which was lit with a hard brilliant light, the costumes were predominantly coloured in shades of red and yellow except Don John who wore 'waspish black and yellow'.

The second temporary proscenium was always both functional and decorative. For the 1913 *King John* and the 1916 *Macbeth* it took the form of a Norman arch. The first of two photographs of *Macbeth* in Matthews's book shows thick pillars supporting the arch over a darkly-shadowed inner courtyard. The second is more brightly lit with a hanging of jagged, horizontal stripes, forming a background and canopy for a simple throne set on the inner stage.[14] The use of curtains to indicate a change of location was obviously considered essential. Actors would move downstage to the apron during the progress of a scene as the tableau curtains fell behind them. The next scene would be set without interrupting the flow of the action. During *The Merchant of Venice* each of Portia's suitors chose from caskets set on the main stage in an alcove formed by grey curtains.

But Shakespeare's narrative movement between Belmont and Venice was maintained by simply playing each alternate Venetian scene on the apron. In Drinkwater's 1916 *Macbeth* the method was probably carried too far.

In the sleep-walking scene, Margaret Chatwin as Lady Macbeth entered from the left upper stage where the doctor and gentlewoman stood, and moved down steps to the main stage. When she reached 'What need we fear who knows it', she moved on to the apron while the doctor and gentlewoman crossed right to stand by the main proscenium as the tableau curtain was lowered. Chatwin completed her scene on the apron and groped her way to exit through the left proscenium door followed by her gentlewoman. The doctor exited through the right door. In the meantime the stage behind was set for the army of the rebel Scottish soldiers. Margaret Chatwin was praised for her performance. On 1 May the *Post* critic wrote of 'a superb and tragical intensity . . . her immobility in the sleep-walking scene concentrated the anguish and passion where movement would have diffused it'. The *Birmingham Mail*, however, commented on the division of the scene: 'this is one of several pieces of stage management which leaves us unconvinced'. Certainly it cannot have been easy for Chatwin to maintain the level of emotional intensity as a large brown curtain descended behind her. In general the over-enthusiastic use of the curtain to distinguish between the two armies in Act V proved very distracting. The play had begun well with the huge shadows of the witches projected on to a gauze. It was a device which Harcourt Williams remembered and copied for his own production of *Macbeth* at the Old Vic in 1930.

On 24 April 1916, the critic of the *Birmingham Daily Post* attempted an assessment of the overall value of the methods of Shakespearian production at the Rep. It came as part of a review, warts and all, of the revivals of *Twelfth Night* and *The Tempest*. He described the productions as:

> particular experiments corrected by experience. In both there is essential fidelity to the full and actual text. In both there is a fine simplicity of theatrical arrangement, a return to the main Elizabethan conditions yet with proper consideration of the advantage and resources of the modern stage, with its improved means of illumination. In both there is an individual attempt to interpret the

spirit of the whole play and each part, and a wise rejection of all the details of by-play, all the clowning and buffoonery which is a legacy of the decadence of the theatre. Tradition has made old comedy into a lumber room, full of the broken and dusty toys of long dead fools.

1. *Measure for Measure* – The Pilgrim Players (1910)

2nd left Margaret Chatwin (*Isabella*); 4th left Bache Matthews; left of centre T. Foden Flint (*Lucio*); 3rd from right Barry Jackson (*Vincentio*); 2nd from right John Drinkwater (*Angelo*)

2. *King John* – The Pilgrim Players (1911)
Kneeling, Barry Jackson (*Bastard*)

4. Margaret Chatwin as Beatrice (1919 and 1920)

3. Ivor Barnard as Shylock (1913 and 1915)

5.   Set for *Love's Labour's Lost* (1919 and 1920)

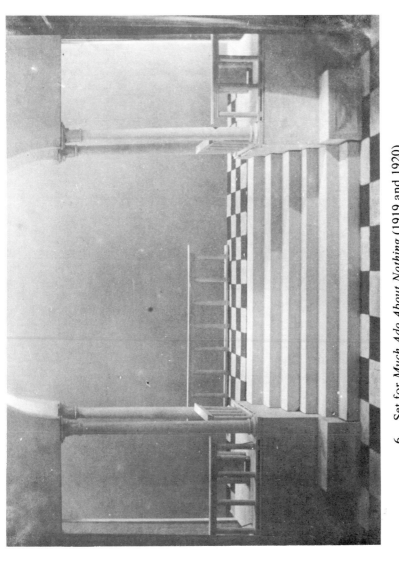

6. Set for *Much Ado About Nothing* (1919 and 1920)

7. *Henry IV Part One* (1920 and 1921)
left on rostrum Osmund Willson (*Falstaff*)

8. Set for Senate scene, *Othello* (1920)
note 'Carpaccio' curtains draped at the back of the stage

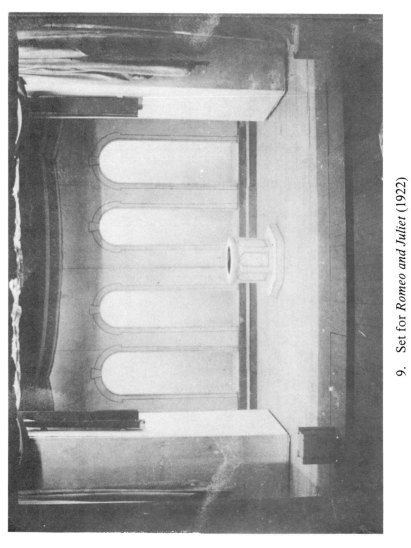

9. Set for *Romeo and Juliet* (1922)

Chapter Five
New Directors, a New Designer and the First London Production

In his comments on the fourteenth-century-inspired design of the Rep's 1919 production of *Much Ado about Nothing*, Crompton Rhodes recognised a 'new English manner' based on deliberate stylisation and the bold use of colour. A week earlier the contrast between the old and the new had been dramatically revealed to Stratford audiences for the Spring Festival at the Shakespeare Memorial Theatre. Alongside extracts from long-standing Benson productions, Nigel Playfair (Bottom in Barker's *A Midsummer Night's Dream*) mounted a dazzling, youthful *As You Like It* with a jaunty conventionalised forest and brilliantly coloured medieval-missal style costumes by Claude Lovat Fraser. Rhodes was staunchly partisan about the overall harmony of the Rep's red and yellow *Much Ado*: 'Compared with it, Mr Lovat Fraser's painstaking decorations . . . are only the efforts of a clever little boy with a paint box' (*Birmingham Daily Post*, 5 May 1919). It was clear, however, that traditional pictorial Shakespeare was becoming increasingly marginalised. The old actor–managers were gradually disappearing from the scene. Tree and Flanagan had both died in 1917 and now Benson was persuaded to relinquish control of the Stratford Festival in favour of Bridges-Adams.

However, thanks to the Rep management's disdain for publicity, very few outside Birmingham knew about Jackson's Shakespeare experiments. Earlier in April 1919, as a Shakespeare birthday tribute, *The Times Literary Supplement* (17 April 1919) published an up-to-date table of English Shakespeare production. The claim to present a comprehensive survey dating back as far as Macready was predictably undermined by several omissions including the work of

71

the Birmingham Repertory Theatre. The Shakespeare Memorial Theatre, and Lilian Baylis's management at the Old Vic which had overseen the production of twenty-seven plays since 1914, were singled out. Miss Horniman with the five productions of her now defunct Manchester Repertory Company was awarded an entry, but not Barry Jackson. The sustained work of six years remained obscure. Indeed even within Birmingham there was local suspicion of the theatre's esoteric principles and amateur origins.

The Rep's national profile had been temporarily raised in February 1919 by the transfer of John Drinkwater's play *Abraham Lincoln* to Nigel Playfair's newly-leased Lyric Theatre, Hammersmith. Its immediate success with London audiences put the Rep on the metropolitan map with 466 performances and led ultimately to an American tour. By the summer, certainly, audiences in Birmingham improved to the extent that it was now possible to introduce a two-week run for each play — a move which relieved the constant pressure and allowed more rehearsal. Even so in July of the following year, W. A. Darlington complained in an article in the *Daily Telegraph* (8 July 1920) that the Rep appeared 'to be bent on doing good by stealth'. After the success of *Abraham Lincoln* the company had quietly vanished back to Birmingham and continued to ignore the necessity to advertise their work. The management seems to have recognised the problem: for the eighth season in September 1920, a discreet publicity notice appeared in the national press and the theatre was made more convivial with the introduction of new refreshment and smoking rooms.

Perhaps the most significant result of the success of *Abraham Lincoln* was the ending of Drinkwater's full-time commitment to Birmingham. His last production of Shakespeare was *The Taming of the Shrew*, complete with the Induction and Christopher Sly, which had its first performance on 15 June 1918. His eventual successor, A. E. Filmer, directed his first Rep production (*Milestones* by Arnold Bennett and Edward Knoblock) in August 1918. Drinkwater retained the official position of General Manager, but when the eighth season opened in 1919, Filmer was known by the new title of Stage Director. As was virtually axiomatic at this time, Filmer had begun his career in theatre as an actor and had occasionally stage-managed at the Rep. The idea of the non-acting director was still relatively new but nonetheless vital to the efficacy of the average short-run provincial repertory programme even though some directors like Playfair appeared from time to time in their own productions. The ideal production process central to the original true repertory concept, with time for careful textual exploration and character development, was expounded by Barker in 1922 in *The Exemplary Theatre*[1] but remained an impossible dream given the crowded short-run schedule. In 1924, quoting Barker's definition of the function of the director 'to suggest, to criticise, to co-ordinate',[2] Bache Matthews clearly saw the task as circumscribed by lack of time. At the Rep in 1920, even with extended runs, the average rehearsal period was twelve days: work beginning at 10 am, followed by an afternoon break for line-learning etc., and then the evening performance. Two of those days were curtailed by matinées. Reading the prompt-books prepared for Filmer's Shakespeare productions one is made aware of careful preparation and scrupulous attention to detail. Reviews of performance, however, highlight the inevitable discrepancy between aspiration and actuality. Matthews describes Filmer as scholarly and fastidious, interested in the psychological dimension of a play and, within the limits of the time at his disposal, concerned to achieve the highest possible degree of finish. Claude Lovat Fraser commented in 1921 that Filmer 'was quick to understand . . . one on whom the subtlest point is never lost'.[3] Under Filmer, the poetic drama which Jackson and Drinkwater had promoted now came from Europe, especially Spain, in José Echegaray's verse melodrama *The Cleansing Stain* and, more successfully in terms of audiences, Martínez Sierra's *The Romantic Young Lady* and *The Two Shepherds* (both translated by Helen and Harley Granville-Barker). Stuart Vinden directed Bjørn Bjørnson's proto-Ibsenite play *The Newly Married Couple*, while Filmer's production of John Masefield's version of Wiers-Jenssen's *The Witch*, with stunning designs by Paul Shelving, drew unusually large audiences for a three-week run followed by two revivals.

Shelving's set for a courtyard in sixteenth-century Bergen, 'buildings and fence a chill greenish-blue, tree-trunks . . . various shades of purple, distant trees black, and behind them an orange sky'[4] was typical of the new young designer Jackson brought to the theatre on Filmer's recommendation during the Christmas holiday of 1919–20. If Barry Jackson's work as a scenic artist is now largely forgotten, Shelving's reputation as one of the most important English designers of this century has also faded with the passing of time. He was a reserved man who appears to have lived entirely for his work, accepting without question the salary he was offered and demanding only that he be allowed to design, without interference, at least three productions a year. He worked for the Rep for more than forty years, resigning only after Jackson's death in 1961. Finlay James, who became his assistant after the Second World War, has recently described his 'gnome-like quality, he looked as if he had come out of the roots of a tree . . . a person of routine who disliked cars or telephones, refused to own them . . . an eighteenth or nineteenth century character'.[5] What his apparent diffidence concealed was a painstaking attention to detail, considerable wit and (which must have been much to Filmer's taste), an implacable pursuit of perfection. It was important to design a set down to the last details of costume, furniture and properties. In 1929, Horace Shipp wrote:

> Fantasy and charm, beauty and purity of form there are in his work with a delight in the details, but nevertheless, a unity and breadth of artistic purpose. No artist can better create a period without slavishly imitating its archaeological facts, and within the limits of the method of decoration, no artist can better interpret a character or the psychic motive of a drama.[6]

Shelving was born Frederick William Severne North at Rowley Regis on 29 October 1888. In 1927 he described how he briefly worked as an actor, walking on in Tree's production of *Henry VIII* in 1911: 'I did not pursue the profession which I only took up with a definite purpose in my mind — to get some inkling from the right side of the footlights of the practical needs of the stage'.[7] In 1905 he began training as a scene painter with the Moody–Manners Opera Companies Ltd. at the Scenic Studio in Hendon. His first commission was to design the scenery and costumes for the Hon. Mrs Alfred Lyttelton's morality play *Dame Julian's Widow*, staged at the Little Theatre in 1913; then for *Kit and the Cockyolly Bird* and *Brer Rabbit and Mr Fox* by Mrs Percy Dearmer, produced at the Royal Court in 1914.

Where Jackson saw stage design in terms of an architectural environment, Shelving's approach was very much that of a scene painter; but frank stylisation was to replace naturalistic back-cloth painting. As Matthews wrote, 'Shelving's scenery never pretends'.[8] Aubrey Beardsley's work with the interplay of flat surfaces and bold, technically precise lines was an early influence, as were the violent images and colours created by Leon Bakst and Alexandre Benois for Diaghilev's Ballets Russes which Shelving would have seen in London. Again Matthews wrote, 'The only thing in colour that he seems unable to achieve is muddiness'.[9] On arrival at the Rep the entire stock of scene-painter's colours was scrapped as Shelving sought to find paint which would yield his ideal range of pure colours. Jackson instructed his new colleague not to be 'too outrageous when you come to Birmingham. Break it to them gently'.[10] For Shelving's first work on *Arms and the Man* in February 1920 there was indeed some mild outrage at the defiantly non-naturalistic blue, yellow and red settings. When Jackson directed and designed *Henry IV Part Two* in 1921 Shelving contributed a costume and mask for Rumour played by Stuart Vinden. The head, like the oriental masks then much admired in wider artistic circles, sported a shock of spiky hair, a huge mouth and teeth and five tongues protruding down the actor's chest. With the addition of gigantic wings, the character resembled a malevolent angel.

It must be admitted, however, that there is some evidence to suggest that Shelving felt constrained by the time-honoured austerities of Rep Shakespeare. As we shall see, conscious restraint in settings sometimes resulted in over-elaborate costuming, and attempts to extend the range of scenic opportunities led to stage-management problems. Filmer's production of *The Merry Wives of Windsor*, presented virtually uncut as a pre-Christmas show in 1920, derived, but as stylised pastiche, from Oscar Asche's typically flamboyant, snow-laden production of the play at the Garrick Theatre in 1911. Shelving designed sets of half-timbered houses in wintertime with the final scene showing a conventionalised distant view of Windsor after a fall of snow. For an audience now unused to flown Shakespearian decor, the sight, through ineptly-closed curtains, of streets and houses ascending into the flies created unlooked-for laughter.

The controversy which *Othello* provoked extended beyond the visual and textual treatment to include the other production choices which made this version of a much performed tragedy highly idiosyncratic. The textual treatment of *Othello* was emphasised in the advance publicity which warned that the performance would begin half an hour earlier than usual at 7pm in order to give the play 'in its entirety'. Such a claim was inevitably open to question and William Archer, who reviewed the production in the *Star* on 7 May, was not only alert to any unacknowledged omissions but also timed the performance. By his reckoning it ran for two hours forty minutes together with two ten-minute intervals. He noticed the removal of the colloquy between Desdemona and Emilia and guessed the additional loss of about sixty lines. In fact, if the prompt-book represents what was actually intended, nearly three hundred lines were cut. Lengthy speeches were pruned, including part of Othello's account of his tales told to Desdemona in I.iii which begins 'wherein of antres vast and deserts idle' and moves on to the 'The Anthropophagi, and men whose heads/Do grow beneath their shoulders'. Inevitably a degree of bowdlerisation was a factor. Iago's goading of Othello to imagine Desdemona in the act of adultery in III.iii ('It were a tedious difficulty, I think/To bring them to that prospect') was cut as were the grossest details of his fabricated account of Cassio's dream. The lines in IV.i were cut:

> *Iago*   Or to be naked with her friend abed
>   An hour or more, not meaning any harm?
> *Othello*   Naked abed, Iago, and not mean harm!

The prompt-book shows that Desdemona's cry in IV.iii 'I cannot say whore/It does abhor me now I speak the word', was cut and then reinstated. The earlier exchange with Othello, the subject of the famous Bensonian 'Notta' joke,[11] remained intact:

> *Othello*   What, not a whore?
> *Desdemona*   No, as I shall be saved

The whole of the verbal battle between Desdemona and Iago on beauty and intelligence in II.i, was considered unnecessary, so that a chance to hear Desdemona's wit pitted against Iago's misogyny was lost. Filmer, it was reported (at a time when women over thirty had only just won the right to vote), was not much interested in the women's argument! The play was certainly not given in 'its entirety' but it was probably the fullest text Archer had ever heard in the theatre. An impression of completeness would have been reinforced by the inclusion of the Herald's speech in II.ii, the scene between the musicians and the clown in III.i, and Desdemona's questioning of the clown in III.iv.

What did irritate Archer was the speed with which the text was delivered. In a second review of the production published on 15 May in the *Illustrated Sporting and Dramatic News*, entitled 'Holus Bolus Shakespeare', he suggested that more cutting might have been preferable: 'to crowd as many words as possible into a given time is to honour Shakespeare in the letter and not in the spirit. Unless common-sense has had its day . . . I cannot doubt that this craze for holus bolus non-stop Shakespeare will presently die out.' It is difficult to know how far this criticism was justified. The charge of gabbling Shakespeare had been levelled at Barker's Savoy actors and it occurs again and again in reviews of the Rep productions throughout their early years. Perhaps it was the familiar problem of under-rehearsal which meant that speed blundered into incoherence. Archer complained of Bensonian-style sketchiness in the *Othello* cast's delivery. But also acting styles were undergoing such a momentous transformation that audiences and even eminent critics found it hard to accept the new fashion. As late as 1929, when Harcourt Williams became director of productions at the Old Vic, he found himself combating the old mannered way of speaking Shakespeare.[12]

All the Birmingham newspaper critics, however, agreed with Archer that Stuart Vinden was physically too slight to play the Moor. Pre-war Othellos had included Lewis Waller, Oscar Asche and Johnston-Forbes Robertson, while in 1920 at the New Theatre in London Matheson Lang was playing the role opposite Arthur Bourchier's Iago. The *Birmingham Mail* even suggested, recalling his performance as the Prince of Morocco, that Barry Jackson should have played the part. The *Post* stated that though Vinden's 'effort was magnificent' he 'could not encompass the tragical grandeur of the declamatory style and he deliberately avoided the realistic . . . the experience of generations has shown that the physical demands of

Othello are inexorable'. A letter to the *Post* on 7 May by one P. T. Cresswell claimed that there was nothing in Shakespeare's text which demands a man of large build. The letter also warned that 'the experience of generations' was not necessarily to be trusted. Matheson Lang writing from London in a letter that was published in the *Post* on 18 May, joined in the debate:

> I, myself, am a tall man of fairly vigorous physique but I have never felt in playing Othello that that was any advantage to me in my portrayal of the role. I have always pictured Othello more as a lithe 'tiger' type . . . undoubtedly the tradition that Othello should be big comes from the fact that the part is of so strenuous and exacting a nature that only a very strong man can possibly give an adequate portrayal of it from start to finish . . . We have many traditions about the characters in the British Theatre that have come down from old actors that are just as wrong as this one and they are nearly all traced to the physiques of the actors who portrayed these roles.

Clearly the challenge to audience preconceptions was such that an objective assessment of Vinden's effectiveness is impossible at this distance in time. But just as the notion of the physical dominance of Othello was jettisoned so the presentation of Iago was modified to avoid either the satanic humourist or the melodramatic villain. Furthermore, the fuller text also meant that a more complex characterisation was possible. Frank Moore played Iago in what Archer considered to be a 'thoroughly competent and effective' performance. Speaking rapidly, without pause for histrionic effect or comic bandinage with the audience, Moore created a plain, blunt humourless soldier. The *Birmingham Mail* critic considered him 'mordant, implacable and even terrifying'. Susan Richmond played Desdemona, not, as some would have preferred, darkly Italianate, but in a blonde wig which obviously made a strong visual contrast with Vinden's Moor. Trained in Benson's company, Susan Richmond had been widely praised for her powerful performance as the reputed witch-wife Ann Pedersdotter in *The Witch*. Her Desdemona was not so much a youthful victim as a mature woman with considerable physical allure. As might be expected, the part of Emilia suited Margaret Chatwin very well and she was particularly impressive in her final scene with Othello. The prompt-book makes clear that she revealed her suspicions of Iago as early as IV.ii, staring hard across a table at her husband as she blamed 'some most villainous knave'.

The emotional intensity of what was publicised as a domestic tragedy was emphasised in the simple curtained conventionality of the setting and dim lighting which suggested candle-lit interiors. The false proscenium incorporated a balcony on either side of the main stage which provided upper and lower entrances. The first two scenes in Venice were played as a continuous sequence in front of grey curtains dropped behind the structure. Brabantio appeared on the right balcony as from an upper window while Iago and Roderigo shouted their news about Desdemona from relative obscurity beneath. After Brabantio's departure with a torch bearer the grey curtains opened several feet to admit Othello. For the third scene in the Venetian senate, the main stage was revealed draped in the Carpaccio tapestry curtains and furnished minimally with two low tables, stools and an elaborately canopied ceremonial throne where the Duke sat with senators on either side. In a new and further development in the Rep's emphasis on obvious conventionality, there were moments during the performance when furniture was set in full view of the audience. At the end of the Senate scene Iago watched the other characters exit through the left balcony door, and then sat down on the Duke's table to talk to Roderigo. Halfway through his speech beginning 'Virtue? A fig!' a servant entered and gestured to Iago to get off the table. Iago shrugged his shoulders and walked downstage right. The servant blew out the candles and then went stage centre to signal for the grey curtains to close in front of him leaving Iago and Roderigo to complete the scene downstage.

The basic full set for Cyprus used a rostrum at the back of the inner stage, reached by a narrow flight of stairs bounded by a bannister. A window was depicted on the stage left back wall. At the end of the play Desdemona's curtained bed was positioned right on the rostrum while the window was lit to suggest moonlight. The chest which contained drapery and Othello's hidden sword was on the main stage below the steps. Jackson's earlier Shakespeare designs had favoured the use of plain-coloured curtains to define acting areas and as we have seen there had been little attempt to emulate the beautiful painted curtains used so successfully by

Norman Wilkinson at the Savoy. As a scene painter of equal stature, Shelving increasingly exploited the decorative opportunities of painted soft scenic-canvas curtains. No photograph has survived but a curtain depicting a street scene in Cyprus was lowered while the herald read out the proclamation from the left balcony. Later it formed the background for Cassio's meeting with Bianca in III.iv.

The first interval came after Cassio's disgrace in II.iv, so the second act of the production concentrated on the two long scenes between Othello and Iago. III.i where Cassio enlists Emilia's help begins with the musicians and here utilised the grey curtains. As Emilia and Cassio left the stage in search of Desdemona, Othello and Iago entered carrying letters and plans for fortifications. The curtains opened for III.iii on to the tapestry-draped stage to discover Desdemona seated at a table holding a lute while Emilia stood beside her. As Cassio pleaded with Desdemona, Othello re-entered still studying the plans, with Iago at his side carrying a sword and sword belt which were placed against a wall. After the women's exit, Othello sat at the table where Emilia had earlier arranged a vase of lilies which stood beside a mirror — personal effects associated with Desdemona which exacerbated Othello's psychological torment.

As Iago's insinuations began to sink in, Othello rose and walked down the right of the stage. Throughout the scene Othello kept moving, constantly crossing and recrossing the stage. When Iago reminded him of Desdemona's deception of her father and Brabantio's charge of witchcraft, Othello sat down suddenly in the chair only to get up almost immediately followed by Iago still talking. Othello picked up the mirror and stood looking at it so that Iago was able to point to his reflection when he reached 'Of her own clime, complexion, and degree'. After Iago's departure Othello sat to deliver his soliloquy 'This fellow's of exceeding honesty', staring again at the mirror when he got to 'Haply, for I am black'. Desdemona entered on the rostrum and came down the stairs to stand close behind her husband as she attempted to bind his head with her handkerchief. She shrank away from him after Othello rose abruptly to stand on the stairs waiting for her to attend into dinner and then faced him on 'I am very sorry that you are not well'. Emilia found the handkerchief on the chair and walked down stage right as Iago, entering from the upper right, went to lean over the plans on the table. Facing him across the table she kept the handkerchief behind her back until he went to grab it and she ran round the chair. Once caught Iago bundled her off up the stairs and came back tossing the handkerchief up in the air on 'Trifles light as air'. As he revealed his plot to the audience they could see Othello standing anguished on the balcony. Iago smelled the handkerchief, folded it and buttoned it into his top pocket as Othello entered upstage left and came down to the pillar where he leant with his face in his hands. Iago watched him from the central opening in the curtain as he spoke:

> ... Not poppy, nor mandragora
> Nor all the drowsy syrups of the world,
> Shall ever medicine thee to that sweet sleep
> Which thou owed'st yesterday.

Minutes later the scene exploded into violence as Othello sprang at Iago forcing him down on 'Villain, be sure thou prove my love a whore'. Iago fought free and ran to get his sword from its place by the wall and threw it down on 'take mine office' and then walked off to the right hand door on 'I'll love no friend, sith love breeds such offence', only to step back as Othello pleaded 'Nay, stay. Thou shouldst be honest'. As the scene continued and Othello became more convinced, he moved around the stage from the right pillar to the table to the left pillar while Iago relentlessly followed. Finally when Othello declared 'I'll tear her all to pieces', he picked up one of the lilies and crushed it in his hand. Perhaps the last line of Sonnet 94 was in Filmer's mind: 'Lilies that fester smell far worse than weeds'.

The prompt-book is extraordinarily detailed, giving an almost move by move account of the production. The stage business, not fussy, but frequently strikingly appropriate, and the simultaneous use of more than one stage level could not form a greater contrast to Drinkwater's carefully studied but austerely static productions. In III.iv when Othello demands Desdemona's handkerchief, Vinden stretched out his hand behind his back waiting for her to place it there. The sequence in IV.i where he overhears Iago and Cassio discussing Bianca was played with Othello hiding behind the tapestry curtains. Sally Beauman records that Bridges-Adams cut this episode because he could not bear the idea of the 'noble Moor' indulging in something so undignified.[13] In V.i, Iago stood hidden by a pillar while Roderigo lay in wait for Cassio behind the grey curtains. As Cassio rushed to the curtains to discover his assailant, Iago crossed upstage to stab him from behind while Othello appeared briefly on the left balcony to assure himself that Cassio had indeed been killed. As Iago dragged Roderigo's body from the stage the grey curtains opened on to the full set and Othello appeared carrying a lamp. After blowing out the lamp and placing it on the stool beside the bed, he opened the bed curtains to kiss his wife. She sighed, woke up, and sat up as Othello moved down the steps and away to the right. As he warned her to make brief prayers, he moved up and then across to the left of the bed in a wide curving walk almost certainly accentuated by the Moorish costume he was now wearing. On Desdemona's 'Talk you of killing?' he went up one step to the left facing her. As he moved closer, she shrank back kneeling on the bed and clutched at him twice as she attempted to defend herself. Finally on the news of Cassio's death she cried 'Alas, he is betray'd, and I undone!' and flung herself face downwards on the pillows. Othello pulled her to face him and threw her down again on her back. As he smothered her with the pillow the prompt-book reads:

> Her left arm is fully extended upwards. Fingers move convulsively.
> At last her arm falls over her face on to her right shoulder, palm up,
> thumb on palm.

In the last moments of Othello's life, he held his sword over his head as in a fencing salute to Gratiano. Then Othello extended his right arm and the sword to the right and lowered it in a gesture of formal resignation.

As mentioned above, for the final scene Vinden changed his Renaissance Venetian dress to full Moorish costume which Shelving, following his usual practice of simulating rich embroidery, decorated with stencilled patterns. It is clear that the costumes created a vivid impression although no details of colours have survived. Othello's everyday European dress was obviously in a paler colour to accentuate his dark skin. In a photograph of Othello and Iago, Vinden's doublet and Venetian breeches are slashed to reveal a brighter fabric beneath. Frank Moore's costume is darker and plainer. Shelving appears to have indulged himself in the women's costumes. Bianca's gown, 'modelled on an authentic engraving of a Florentine courtesan of the period', was recorded as very striking but evidently too elaborate. Archer complained that Susan Richmond's dress with a long full train would have been better suited to Queen Elizabeth I. From the stage directions in the prompt-book which frequently direct the actors to make broad sweeping movements around the stage it seems possible that spatially the production aimed at an semblance of grandeur which would counterpoint the simplicity of the basic design.

Reviews made only passing references to the supporting roles. Archer briefly singled out Osmund Willson's Brabantio, Oliver Johnstone's Cassio and Eric Messiter's Roderigo, but there is no indication as to how the characters were presented. The play was given an initial twenty performances and then a further nine at the end of May. But the audacity of the directorial approach, as well as the painstaking preparation of the overall production, make it a classic example of Rep Shakespeare. The obvious shortcomings were a direct result of the pressures and constraints of the short-run system. In the first four months of 1920, Vinden for example played Martin in *The Witch*, Bluntschli in *Arms and the Man*, directed *The Newly Married Couple*, played in Carrol Aikins's tragic allegory about North American Red Indians *The God of Gods*, and, while rehearsing Othello, played Berowne in the revival of *Love's Labour's Lost*. Such a punishing schedule must have been emotionally and intellectually enormously stimulating and utterly exhausting. In 1921, just before he was due to take up the post of Producer at the Liverpool Playhouse, Vinden nearly died of acute septicaemia and was left permanently disabled. In 1922, Filmer took six months' leave because of exhaustion and finally resigned from the Rep at the end of that year.

What is also obvious, however, as the new decade dawned, was that the Rep's management was shifting into a higher gear. The amateur origins and homegrown isolation were receding into the past. Although Jackson provided designs for revivals of *Twelfth Night* in 1922 and *The Two Gentlemen of Verona* in 1925, his production of *Henry IV Part One* first staged in November 1920 and then revived in tandem with *Part Two* in April 1921 was effectively the last major Shakespearian project for which he had personal directorial and design responsibility. It was an ambitious enterprise with the visual objective of stylised medievalism confidently publicised. The distinguished antiquary Alfred Rodway was called on to ensure accuracy in the various heraldic devices emblazoned on the shields and banners, and backcloths contributed to an illuminated missal effect. The battle of Shrewbury was fought against a tiny conventionalised view of the walled town of Shrewsbury and there was also a cloth of old London which looked across the Thames from the edge of a wharf to the gables and turrets of the city. Essentially the design was as uncluttered as before but some of the early austerity had gone.

The use of alternating acting areas had an extra refinement which complemented Shakespeare's narrative and conceptual technique. The inner proscenium was painted to resemble the decorative timber frame of a medieval house, with windows depicted on the deep bridge of the frame. The upper stage was further divided into two curtained halves. When the left curtain was drawn back a palace setting was revealed, with a simple red background spangled with gold lilies, and a centrally-placed throne. On the right a tavern scene was represented by plain wooden furniture placed in front of a small fireplace and mantleshelf set with pewter plates and jugs. A narrow flight of stairs with a wooden bannister led to an upper entrance. Falstaff was first discovered asleep in a large wooden chair beside a table. In *Part Two* the same scheme was used to suggest Warksworth castle and Shallow's house. The design seems unnecessarily restricting for such a small stage but Bache Matthews insists that in practice all proceeded very smoothly.[14] Once the scene location was defined by the appropriate half of the stage, the action spilled forward on to the lower acting area and for the Gadshill robbery and the Battle of Shrewbury the entire upper stage was used. The only objection was to the permanent wooden post. As we have already seen E. H. Baughan identified Falstaff's ironic choric role through Osmund Willson's performance and his initial resistance to the one-sided effect was overcome as the whole stage was utilised. The critic of the *Birmingham Gazette* (29 November 1920) pointed out 'What is vastly more important from an artistic point of view is that this halving principle helped enormously to bring out the dual nature of Prince Hal's character and to throw into strong relief the contrast between the make-believe and the real heart to heart talk between royal father and prodigal son'.

For performance on the apron, the tableau curtains were occasionally looped up on rings to form an inverted V-shaped opening where, for example, the throne was placed for the King's interview with his son in III.ii. For this scene Baughan complained of crowded grouping within the opening and poor lighting. However in *Part Two* a similar technique was used for the staging of the King's death. IV.iv began with the entry of the King with his courtiers and younger sons on to the apron. As Henry collapsed and the action moved into the next scene, the curtain formed the same opening to reveal a bed. There was a cushion set beside the bed where Gloucester placed the crown and where Hal sat for his final talk with his father. In theory the sequence as shown in the prompt-book looks remarkably smooth and suggests that the transition to the Jerusalem chamber did not break the mood created by the sense of approaching death.

After *Henry IV* Shakespeare production was taken over by H. K. Ayliff, who was appointed Stage Director when Filmer finally departed in 1922. The man who directed the British premières of *Back to Methuselah!* and Georg Kaiser's *Gas* as well as the earliest British commercial production of *Six Characters in Search of an Author* in his own translation,[15] nursed the early performances of Laurence Olivier, Ralph Richardson, Cedric Hardwicke and Gwen Ffrangçon-Davies and directed all the Rep's productions of Shakespeare in modern dress in the 1920s, is now rarely mentioned in standard works of reference on the history of British theatre. Even J. L. Styan's account of Rep Shakespeare awards Ayliff a secondary role. Ayliff does, however, occasionally feature in theatrical biographies, usually as an object of both awe and terror. John Harrison, who along with Paul Scofield was directed by Ayliff in the 1944 *The Winter's Tale* which was his last Rep Shakespeare, remembered him 'like an Old Testament divinity . . . about 7 ft tall and as bald as an egg'.[16] His anger — James Bridie described him as having 'a tongue like a file'[17] — permanently blighted many a nervous young actor's career. In 1953 Ralph Richardson remembered him as a:

> Weird . . . daddy longlegs of a man. And these long legs shot him seven foot or more into the air. And there he lived above our heads in a stormy region of his own . . . But those who had the wit and nerve could often make a call that would expose a bluff.[18]

Those actors of wit and nerve who survived testified to Ayliff's ability to shape and refine new plays and to train new actors, especially those like Cedric Hardwicke whose talent was not immediately obvious.

Born in 1871 in South Africa, Henry Kiell Ayliff first studied art in London and Paris and then trained as an actor with Hermann Vezin. In some respects Vezin's public persona, scholarly, fastidious but ostensibly lacking warmth, was reflected in Ayliff's reticence. He was fiercely professional but rarely gave interviews, content as the company's fame grew to bow to Jackson as spokesman for production policy. His acting roles had included the part of Juggins in *Fanny's First Play* where even in the rehearsal period Shaw noted Ayliff's capacity for independent characterisation.[19] He first appeared at the Rep as an actor in October 1921 playing the priest Don Antonio in Barker's translation of Sierra's *Two Shepherds*. When exhaustion forced Filmer to take temporary leave in 1922, Ayliff started to direct a series of productions which included Ibsen's *Ghosts* and Harold Chapin's *New Morality*. Plays were studied carefully and moves plotted in advance. Matthews noted that Ayliff was 'a happy combination of Jackson's vigour and Filmer's delicacy, as well as being an indefatigable worker'.[20] Like Shelving, he was interested in period furniture and costume. His son David Ayliff has suggested that it was his father's early training in portrait painting in landscape, combined with an acute understanding of colour, which made his collaboration with Shelving so successful. Ralph Richardson praised Ayliff's skill with lighting and 'the dazzling, searching, diamond coloured illumination he poured upon his stage'[21] — although as we shall see this was a skill that seems to have been acquired after much trial and error. David Ayliff explained that his father used pink and blue-toned gelatines to produce warm and cool light directionally so that 'the natural modelling of actors' faces and draped costumes and curtains could be brought out, instead of being flattened . . . his subtle blending of colours produced the nearest possible imitation of natural daylight so that the colours of Paul Shelving's painted scenery and costumes were seen by the audiences as the designer intended'.[22] Gary O'Connor described the final effect achieved by Shelving and Ayliff: 'The total impression was of careful and unobtrusive quality — an ordinary appearance which on close scrutiny one saw was fashioned from the most expensive materials'.[23]

The events which led up to the staging of Ayliff's 1922 production of *Romeo and Juliet* at the Regent Theatre in 1924 were typical of the weird mixture of artistic prestige and poor local esteem which would continue to dog Jackson's company. The 1922 production received the usual sparse but on the whole appreciative reviews. The London revival provoked by comparison an avalanche of critical comment, some from the most distinguished theatre critics of the day, and all demonstrating the wide range of response which reflects the individual experience and prejudices of each member of an audience. In Birmingham, the years after 1920 were amazingly creative. Having proved that scenically refined Shakespeare could be aesthetically satisfying, Jackson turned his attention to opera, that other great bastion of grandiose production values, with a small-scale production of *Così Fan Tutti* in the summer of 1920. Three more followed a year later: *Il Matrimonio Segreto* by Cimarosa, Donizetti's *Don Pasquale* and Rutland Boughton's *The Immortal Hour*, which was first composed for the Glastonbury Festival. Like Playfair's 1920 revival of John Gay's *The Beggar's Opera*, which brought audiences flocking to the Lyric Theatre for an eighteenth-century revival, Boughton's new English music–drama with its romantic fairy story, haunting melodies and Shelving's beautiful atmospheric sets immediately captured the imagination of audiences first in Birmingham and then in London when the production transferred to the Regent Theatre on 13 October 1922. In 1923, which also saw a second Rep company touring the country, a modern-dress production of *Cymbeline* and the colossal enterprise of the British première of Shaw's *Back to Methuselah!* attracted international attention to Birmingham. Local audiences, however, seemed if anything further alienated by critical acclaim and radical experiment. Audiences dwindled until a poor response to Kaiser's *Gas* with superb expressionistic sets by Shelving provoked Jackson into announcing the closure of his Birmingham base. On 9 February 1924 there was a last performance of a revival of Eden Phillpott's *The Farmer's Wife*. On 18 February the company opened at the Royal Court with *Back to Methuselah!* which was replaced by *The Farmer's Wife*: a production which would run for over a thousand performances. At the Regent, a Boughton music-drama, *Bethlehem*, directed by Jackson, was followed by another popular revival of *The Immortal Hour. Romeo and Juliet* opened on 24 May.

By 1924 in London at any rate (provincial touring production was another matter), simply-staged Shakespeare in virtually full text was not going to create a great controversy. During the run of *Romeo and Juliet*, two other companies were also playing Shakespeare according to much the same well-established policy. Robert Atkins' Old Vic Company played, by courtesy of C. B. Cochran, at the New Oxford Theatre, while Bridges-Adams' New Shakespeare Company came from Stratford to the King's Theatre. Debate in the mid-twenties focused far more on style and decorative innovation. Indeed one review of the Regent production compared Shelving's usual semi-permanent sets, alternating with curtains, to the techniques deployed in the intimate revues which Cochran in particular had made so fashionable. Textual purity was no longer such a major issue, although several seasoned London playgoers admitted they had never seen such a complete *Romeo and Juliet* staged. Only the London prompt-book, which shows the excision of about two hundred and fifty-five lines, has survived and the assumption that the treatment in 1922 and 1924 was the same has to be made with some caution. However in Birmingham in 1922 the contrast between the Rep's version and older productions, which had emphasised almost exclusively the lyricism of the central love story, was strong enough to prompt the critic of the *Birmingham Mail* (29 May 1922) to write that the Rep had done 'nothing more creditable than their unbotched unpretentious rendering of Shakespeare's lovely tragedy . . . To most of us on Saturday it was a new play'. For Crompton Rhodes, writing in the *Birmingham Daily Post* (29 May 1922) lyricism was now firmly yoked to the emotional and social realism inherent in the play as a whole: '*Romeo and Juliet* is poetry and beautiful poetry, but also it is a "slice of life" as decidedly a "slice" as any modern tragedy by Ibsen . . . it is a story of medieval Italy. Not sentimentalised out of all semblance of life but showing one phase of humanity in its richness and completeness'. For Rhodes, the production gave fuller realisation to characters like Alan Bland's 'gentlemanly' Paris and Orlando Barnett's 'dignified, benevolent and ineffective' Friar Laurence. The Nurse, played by Isabel Thornton, seems to have benefited most. Rhodes approved her adoption of an air of middle age and middle class comfort 'a rather shallow and garrulous good nature'. In London, however, when the part was played by Barbara Gott (famous for her washerwoman and 'coal-black mammy' impersonations), opinion varied. Many admired a warm, straightforward characterisation while others found her too ladylike and wanted more coarse good humour. The *Spectator* review (31 May 1924) objected to 'severe' cuts in her I.iii speech 'Surely our stomachs are not too squeamish for its honest grossness'. In fact Ayliff, in a strikingly unbowdlerised prompt-text, cut only the character's prolonged account of weaning the infant Juliet 'When it did taste the wormwood on the nipple/Of my dug'. But at the same time there were also a few complaints about the length of the evening. In Birmingham with a 7.30pm start the performance lasted for just over three hours with one interval of ten minutes. In London with a fashionable curtain-up at 8.15pm, the audience found themselves at 11pm with an act and a half to go. The critic of *The Sunday Times* would have happily abandoned text, especially the first long soliloquy of Friar Laurence spoken now by Campbell Gullan. This was another performance which divided critics: the engaging, quietly-humorous friar enjoyed by some was a misconceived doddering pantaloon for others. Christopher St John, writing in *Time and Tide* (6 June 1924) about a text which she felt, for all its completeness, had been dwindled into a 'Babes in the Wood' tale, was clear that 'Half a loaf well baked is to be preferred to a whole one uncooked'.

There were obviously technical problems at the Regent which may have contributed to the half-cooked impression. The pre-production period was rushed, with designs delivered at the last minute and the leading lady completing some of her own costumes. Gielgud describes an unnerving final rehearsal conducted behind a lowered safety curtain.[24] Lighting was problematic with cues missed on the first night and some scenes possibly underlit (obscured faces also provoked complaint in Birmingham). The *Manchester Guardian* (24 May 1924), commenting on 'the fashionable horror of footlights', objected to the 'side-lighting' which compelled the actors to move into 'the livid glare of a baby search light and back into the gloom'. Shelving's original design had to be considerably adapted to the demands of a much larger theatre — the Regent's audience capacity was 1,380 — but it is worth assuming that the basic aim as announced in the London press in April 1924 to create 'a bright, colourful and warm ensemble' and 'to give the play in as youthful an atmosphere as possible with an air of simplicity and sincerity' (*Morning Post*, 24 April 1924) was carried over from Birmingham. In 1922, for the Rep stage, Shelving created the effect of a sunlit cloister against a bright sky with a row of yellow (or white; depending on which review is to be believed) arches ranged behind two steps stretching the width of the inner stage. Entrances set halfway up the deep false proscenium and facing out to the stage were draped with plain-coloured hangings for scenes located in the public square, which were then changed for Capulet's feast. A small hexagonal well formed a centrepiece in the square while canvas-covered frames supplied seating. For the balcony scene a square structure with an arched balustrade, corresponding to the taller arches formed by the supporting pillars, was placed against the right wall of the false proscenium. Both plain and decorative curtains were used for front scenes, which included Juliet's first appearance with her mother and nurse, and the friar's cell. A 'Verona street curtain' is illustrated in Matthews' book: 'pink buildings relieved with red, black and white, standing before an ultramarine river. The sails of the ship are yellow. The sky is turquoise blue'.[25] At the Regent the curtain for I.iv, where Romeo and his friends prepare to gate-crash Capulet's feast, depicted the silhouette of buildings and hills against an early evening sky with a setting sun.

In Birmingham the design for the second half of the play seems to have been less successful but no accurate record has survived. There were complaints about poor lighting and noisy scene-shifting especially during the final-act transition to Juliet's tomb; and in both revivals there appears to have been more specific scenic localisation than was usual in Rep Shakespeare. In 1922 Crompton Rhodes published a book analysing the most recent theories about Elizabethan stagecraft and included an appendix which described the Elizabethan/Victorian scenic compromise which he felt had evolved successfully at the Rep.[26] In his review of the Regent production he remarked that the *Romeo and Juliet* design was the least representative of the Rep's methods, but nonetheless found the London set an improvement on the Birmingham version. Inevitably in London the set was far more massively built although still very plain and, of course, there was no cyclorama to light for outdoor scenes. Some critics objected to the use of curtains for exterior scenes, clearly preferring more specific indication of outdoors — especially in the balcony scene where even a token orchard tree was denied them. There was no separate balcony, instead a permanent tower with three arched windows where different-coloured cloths defined location was built at the back of the inner stage and did duty as a building facing into Verona square, as Capulet's feasting hall (where it became a musicians' gallery) and as the balcony outside Juliet's bedchamber. As for the most important balcony in dramatic literature, a review in the *Outlook* (31 May 1924) compared it here to an ugly, impracticable land-battleship. Another (*Referee*, 25 May 1924), referring to its blank high walls, described it as 'Gordon Craigery run mad' and claimed that patrons at the back of the circle had to bend over sideways or even come out 'and squat on the floor' to catch a sight of the lovers.

Nevertheless, other reviews concentrated on Shelving's use of additional colour: in particular praising the evocation of Juliet's chamber (set within enclosing curtains above steps on the inner stage) which was draped in scarlet and gold and various shades of blue. As with *Othello* Shelving reserved his visual extravagance for the fifteenth-century, Carpaccio/Botticelli-inspired costumes. The Nurse in both revivals looked enormous (Barbara Gott, it was suggested, might have worn less petticoats), in a vigorously-patterned striped dress and a huge stiff winged cap over a tightly-bound wimple. All the young men's short tunics and hose had similar bold patterns with an assortment of accessories which included vivid draped cloaks, tasselled square purses, long elegant daggers and flat-topped decorated hats. The older men wore elaborately-stencilled gowns with long sleeves. In *Early Stages* Gielgud complained that the gold paint used for the stencilling 'smelt abominably . . . My wig was coal-black and parted in the middle. Wearing an orange makeup and a very low-necked doublet I look, in the photographs, a mixture of Rameses of Egypt and a Victorian matron'.[27] Certainly his first costume did generate some adverse comment. However, audiences loved the beautiful dresses worn by Gwen Ffrangçon-Davies. From press interviews given at the time, it is clear that she was very happy to scurry through six costume changes despite the additional burden of a London heatwave. For Capulet's dance, she wore a voluminous green dress stencilled in gold and belted over a gold petticoat, with a 'primavera' wreath of rose petals and seed pearls over her long curled auburn wig. Her dress for her marriage to Romeo was white, stencilled with a blue pineapple pattern, and she was laid on her tomb in the gold-coloured gown chosen for her wedding to Paris.

For some, the exquisite quality of the design contributed to doubts about the overall tone of the production. Desiring something more earthy, with more stress on the bawdy, Francis Birrell in the *Nation and Atheneum* complained of 'a faint aroma of Liberty silk'. For others with more conservative views on Shakespeare production, the cool efficiency, even angularity of the set (which Gielgud disliked), seemed to reflect the perceived lack of lush romanticism traditionally associated with past performances. This was a production of a much-loved play which risked alienating those with long-cherished imaginative engagement with the central protagonists and strong views on how they should be played. Certainly the more or less complete text meant that Ayliff was able to delineate quite carefully the full social and personal landscape of the play, in particular giving full weight to the family feud which precipitates the tragedy. The family groups were colour-coded in distinctive blue costumes for the Montagues and red and orange for the Capulets. After the introductory Chorus, the play began with Verona bells summoning the people to church. Lady Montague and Lady Capulet moving from opposite entrances with accompanying followers met below the well for a silent confrontation which led to the retreat of Lady Montague and the triumphant passage of her foe.

However there was a considerable divergence of opinion on the effectiveness of the subsequent crowd and fight scenes. The *Stage* praised the fights, which Ashley Dukes in the *Illustrated Sporting and Dramatic News* considered inept, while Crompton Rhodes described people pouring on and off the stage 'like ants in a disturbed nest' but lacking fully-realised engagement in the action. Dukes, a committed advocate of avant-garde European production values, objected to the 'mixture of style and realism' wanting the new simplified settings which had swept away 'the dreary old procession of painted scenes' to lead directors away from naturalistic acting and stage business.

Although there was no formally-stated directorial policy, there are signs of a transition to a more naturalistic delivery of the verse which would have major implications for the next phase of production experiment. The critic of the *Daily Mirror* (24 May 1924) wondered in the course of his review 'whether we shall ever cure some of our actors of trying to put a conversational "snap" into Shakespearean lines'. Gielgud later wrote of Campbell Gullan, whose work he admired, that he had no experience of Shakespearian acting, and so wrote out his speeches in modern prose before learning the verse.[28] Francis Birrell complained bitterly that Scott Sunderland as Mercutio delivered the Queen Mab speech 'as a series of happy thoughts, punctuated at intervals with "cheers and laughter" from his admiring companions'. But again Sunderland's performance divided opinion. Ivor Brown, in the *Saturday Review* (31 May 1924) rather liked his 'taurine' approach, while the *Manchester Guardian* noted his 'rough-edged, vigorous work'. Hubert Griffith, with direct reference to Gwen Ffrangçon-Davies's technique, maintained in a long *Observer* review (25 May 1925) that the verse needed only to be spoken, not acted. He objected to her treatment of the 'Gallop apace' speech which she took 'slowly and brokenly and with interminable pauses', and he also complained that Ayliff had allowed her to cry out with raised arms 'but farewell compliment' in the balcony scene, a phrase which Griffith considered an aside to be delivered quietly.

In fact within the parameters of the production's insistence on the extreme youth of the lovers, this Juliet was very much the actress's creation. Ayliff, she maintained, staged the play because he felt she could perform the role and then she was left to work it out.[29] Over thirty by 1922, she deployed a range of vocal and physical tricks, including childlike gestures and little cries of fear and excitement, to portray a very young girl. In London audiences were confronted (though many did not realise it) with a mature Juliet acting young and a very inexperienced, physically gauche Romeo in the nineteen-year old John Gielgud. The Romeo in Birmingham, Ion Swinley, whose work with the Rep dated back to 1914 and included Caliban in 1916 and a much-praised Orsino in Ayliff's 1922 *Twelfth Night*, was more her match in both age and technique. Crompton Rhodes wrote of his Romeo 'I never hope to see a better . . . the easy manly, common sense manner of his talk with Mercutio, the lyrical ecstacy of his colloquies with Juliet, the terrible anguish, changing to implacable resolution of his discourse with Friar Laurence — it was beyond reproach'. The role of Étain in *The Immortal Hour* had brought Gwen Ffrangçon-Davies in 1921 from Glastonbury to Birmingham and security as a contracted member of the Rep company. The critic of the *Birmingham Gazette* (29 May 1922) stated 'She was a real Juliet — a Shakespeare's Juliet — in that she represented a young girl, not a grown woman. She was virginal, not "vampish". Her voice, a singer's voice, was beautifully used, and one greatly admired the management of the soliloquies, which seemed to be (as they should be) nothing but thoughts uttered aloud'.

In 1924, *The Stage* reminded readers of William Poel's emphasis on the extreme youth of the lovers in his production with the adolescent Esmé Percy and Dorothy Minto at the Royalty in 1905, but for the most part reviews evoked memories of past performances of lyric intensity. The tall, striking Juliet of Phyllis Neilson-Terry at the New Theatre in 1911 was recalled as an example of an actress of only eighteen who nonetheless embodied the powerful emotional maturity of someone much older. In *Early Stages* Gielgud is engagingly frank about his inexperience and nervousness and indeed quotes the most memorable comment on his performance. A review in the *New Age* acknowledged that he had 'a good voice, a pleasant face and a useful figure' but 'the most meaningless legs imaginable . . . perhaps six months of melodrama at, say, the Bordesley Palace, Birmingham would make an actor of him.

Anyhow, Mr Ayliff never will' (29 May 1924). Although some reviews accused him of effeminacy, Ashley Dukes was amongst those who were kinder and more acute 'Here is an actor of possibilities — one who can be moulded, without being lifeless clay in the producer's hands. He seemed to me to be feeling his own way through the part with a sensitive perception'. One or two reviews found him too self-absorbed, while the *Evening News* made an observation which, now with hindsight, looks prophetic 'This was Romeo looking introspectively at Romeo rather than Romeo himself . . . There was more than a touch of the traditional Hamlet' (23 May 1924).

The more knowledgeable critics recognised Gwen Ffrangçon-Davies's technical achievement. By 1924 London had seen her Étain and her Eve in *Back to Methuselah!* as well as her performance as the Queen in the Phoenix Society's production of Marlowe's *Edward II*. Ashley Dukes saluted her creative skills: 'a woman, at least, who draws a character and paints a portrait' but nevertheless, for him she failed: '[Juliet's] youthfulness needs no physical stress . . . she must dominate her father's house with the air of a great lady'. This of course was an extreme view: a more general perception was that she was too English. Herbert Farjeon wrote in the *Weekly Westminster* (31 May 1924) 'It has been well said that the purity of Juliet is not the purity of snow but of fire. And this is where Miss Gwen Ffrangçon-Davies failed. She was never Southern. She was never alight'. The majority, however, agreed with Ivor Brown 'Unripeness is all':

> With a masterly rhetorician as Juliet, the play becomes a gorgeous noise . . . But Miss Davies elaborates the sadness at the expense of the song . . . has just the quality of heart-breaking childhood . . . You forget the crowds and colour of Verona, the Italianate passions, and brilliance of Renaissance life. You see instead a sufferer who might be an English school-miss (only she moves with such beauty that this could hardly be) and you remember that *Romeo and Juliet* is a play and not a pageant or a symphony . . . composed for the benefit of a virtuoso.

It was the playing of the potion scene which left the deepest impression. The *Daily Telegraph* remarked that 'her line "If all else fail, myself have power to die" reminded one oddly of Peter Pan's

"To die would be an awfully big adventure"'. The review in the *Manchester Guardian* stated: 'when in the potion scene Juliet cries "I'll call them back again to comfort me", Miss Davies gave to this line the full terror of a child who has woke suddenly in the dark. It was far more than "Romeo I drink to thee" the pivot of her performance'. Several reviews recalled Ellen Terry's 1919 performance as the Nurse: her last great role. Years before, Gwen Ffrangçon-Davies had been taken by her mother to speak the potion speech to Irving's Juliet. Terry had commended the aspiring actress, but advised her not to cry in that scene: 'Juliet is beyond tears'.[30]

The Birmingham Repertory Company was now firmly established in metropolitan consciousness. Back in Birmingham the Civic Society had succeeded in drumming up enough support to persuade Jackson to re-open the theatre. *The Seal Woman*, a folk-opera by Mrs Kennedy Fraser and Granville Bantock, had its first performance on 27 September 1924. On 22 November Ayliff directed a revival of *The Two Gentlemen of Verona* and on 11 April 1925 Stuart Vinden directed *Love's Labour's Lost*. But both productions represented the end of a era. Early in 1925, Jackson announced that he would work permanently in both London and Birmingham to exploit the Rep's 'artistic capital'. Part of that capital, yet to be fully exploited, was the 1923 modern-dress production of *Cymbeline* which had aroused a great deal of interest. It was in this direction that Jackson and Ayliff turned for further experiments with Shakespeare. The next chapter will go back to 1923 to discuss the origins of a major venture which would have profound repercussions for the future of twentieth-century Shakespeare production.

10. *Romeo and Juliet* (1922)
Gwen Ffrangçon-Davies as Juliet and Isobel Thornton as the Nurse

12. E Stuart Vinden as Othello (1920)

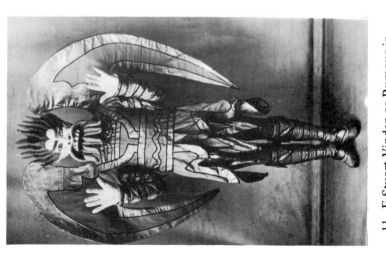

11. E Stuart Vinden as Rumour in
Henry IV Part Two (1921)

13. *Romeo and Juliet* (Regent Theatre, 1924)

3rd left Charles Vane (*Capulet*); centre Gwen Ffrangçon-Davies (*Juliet*); seated 2nd from right Marie Housley (*Lady Capulet*); extreme right John Gielgud (*Romeo*)

Theatre Museum

14. *Hamlet* (Kingsway Theatre, 1925)

Dorothy Massingham (*Gertrude*); Colin Keith-Johnston (*Hamlet*); Frank Vosper (*Claudius*)

Syndication International

15. *All's Well That Ends Well* (1927)
Martin Walker (*Bertram*) and Jane Welsh (*Diana*)

16. *Macbeth* (Royal Court Theatre, 1928)
Joan Pereira (*Second Witch*), Muriel Aked (*First Witch*), Una O'Connor (*Third Witch*),
Eric Maturin (*Macbeth*), Marshall Sheppard (*Banquo*)

Theatre Museum

17. *The Taming of the Shrew* (Royal Court Theatre, 1928)
Foreground: Ernest Stidwell (*Pedant*), Edward Chapman (*Grumio*), Frank Moore (*Vincentio*), Muriel Hewitt (*Bianca*), Chris Castor (*Widow*), Eileen Beldon (*Katharine*), Scott Sunderland (*Petruchio*) Upstage top right, Ralph Richardson (*Tranio*)

18. A company read-through in the Rep foyer (1926)

Standing: Andrew Churchman, Dorothy Hall, Charles Leighton, Margaret Chatwin, Phyllis Percy, Edward Chapman, Dorothy Black, Arthur Blanch, H. K. Ayliff (plus wig!), Stringer Davis Seated: Ralph Richardson, Muriel Hewitt, Isabel Thornton

Chapter Six
'With Shakespeare to Savile Row': the First Modern-Dress Productions

In 1928 in an article aptly titled 'With Shakespeare to Savile Row', H. K. Ayliff summed up his approach to modern-dress Shakespeare by quoting G. C. Lichtenberg's response to Garrick's Hamlet played in 'modern French fashion':

> I think then, when our modern dress in a play does not offend the sensitive dignity of our scholastic learning, we ought by all means to retain it. Our French dress-coats have long since attained to the dignity of a skin, and their folds have the significance of personal traits and expressions, and all the wrestling and bending and fighting and falling in a strange costume we may understand, but we do not feel.[1]

'The significance of personal traits and expressions' was important to Ayliff as pre-eminently a director of modern plays; especially the didactic, stylised naturalism of Shaw. Indeed it was to the insights and techniques derived from naturalistic modern drama that Ayliff turned when he came to direct Shakespeare in modern dress. In 1928, after four productions, he stated firmly that 'Shakespeare was a modern author'.

Precisely why Ayliff and Jackson started the modern-dress experiments is not clear. Jackson had certainly toyed with the idea for some time. In 'Producing the Comedies' he makes a passing reference to a production by Reinhardt of Molière in modern dress. Reinhardt had indeed begun to experiment with shifting period setting. In 1919 at the Grosses Schauspielhaus in Berlin, he directed Alexander Moissi in a semi-modern-dress *Hamlet*.[2] Discussing the Rep's forthcoming modern-dress *Cymbeline* in a *Birmingham Daily*

Post article on 14 April 1923, R. Crompton Rhodes mentioned an earlier project to mount a private performance of *Twelfth Night* with Malvolio dressed as William the Waiter in *You Never Can Tell*. But there was also the specific problem of staging *Cymbeline*. In 1928 Ayliff described the difficult debate with Shelving as to what period would be most suitable: 'There was some strong and valid reason against using every period we suggested. I maintained that period did not matter at all; whereat Shelving retorted that such being the case we might as well do it in modern dress'.[3] Jackson was fond of relating the appealing story of watching impoverished local school children perform the mechanicals' scenes from *A Midsummer Night's Dream*. In his account in 'Producing the Comedies' the experience takes on the same momentous significance as William Poel's *Measure for Measure*. They: 'appeared in their worn everyday clothes, carrying the tools of their trade, their midday meals in pudding basins wrapped up in bandanna handkerchiefs . . . the whole thing became startlingly alive and vibrant'.[4]

Projects aimed at returning the production of Shakespeare to something resembling Elizabethan staging conditions had continued to develop since Poel's 1881 production of the First Quarto of *Hamlet*. In 1921 Nugent Monck opened his amateur Maddermarket Theatre in Norwich expressly to perform Elizabethan plays in an Elizabethan-style theatre. But as Jackson himself knew, quoting a comment of Bridges-Adams, 'It was impossible to Elizabethanise your audience'.[5] Poel's dream of creating 'the realism of an actual event at which the audience assisted'[6] seemed as far away as ever. Even Poel in his last years seemed to move away from his absolutist stance and his eccentric use of costume in his later productions may reflect not so much wilful perversity, as a desire to express something more fundamental about Shakespeare's characters. As we shall see he very much approved of modern-dress Shakespeare. But in a speech given in 1920 called 'Literature and the Drama', Jackson rejected dogmatic Elizabethanism:

> This way of working appears to me to savour of the dilettante, the precious. By making a hard and fast line of a distinct return to a bygone period we hamper progress which is after all what we live for. It is metaphorically speaking surrounding a live and vital thing with a

shroud. If the artist of today is to be of value his work must be visionary of today and tomorrow and not of yesterday.[7]

In general this speech is interesting because Jackson laid before his audience many of the basic principles which governed his theatrical practice. He explored what he termed the 'composite art' of the theatre, distinguishing great literature from great drama by the vital non-verbal dimensions of sound, movement and colour which assist in the theatrical re-telling of a story. In the process he touched on the conspicuous failure of recent would-be dramatists to produce good poetic drama precisely because they ignored the extra needs and disciplines imposed by the theatre. He was anticipating another issue which was to be raised by modern-dress Shakespeare. In debating whether it was appropriate to speak Shakespeare's verse in a modern setting, critics also asked whether it was now possible for modern dramatists to move out of the rut of naturalistic prose drama to create new poetic forms. In 1920, despite the strenuous efforts of theatres like the Rep to promote poetic drama, the prospects seemed remote. The plays of Yeats had achieved only limited recognition and, after several experiments with verse drama, John Drinkwater had turned to prose for his one major success, *Abraham Lincoln*; his only other commercially popular play was a rural comedy in the manner of Eden Phillpotts, *Bird in Hand*, produced in 1927.

In 1923, the tenth anniversary of the founding of the Rep and the tercentenary of the publication of the First Folio, Jackson probably felt the need to produce something special and as always was restless for progress. Paul Shelving may also have needed a change of approach. In a review of *The Two Gentlemen of Verona* in 1924, Crompton Rhodes acknowledged Shelving to be the best scenic artist then working in the English theatre. But he went on to complain about a design which 'perversely dominates the production . . . with a little cramped makeshift setting; atrociously lighted' (*Birmingham Daily Post*, 24 November 1924). The historical eccentricities of *Cymbeline* meant that the play proved highly resistant to Jackson's usual method of finding an ideal visual correlative. Modern dress was to give Shelving an opportunity to exploit his love of period detail and his gift for controlled anarchy of

99

colour and style in a way that was both witty and appropriate.

This first experiment, however, was relatively simple. *Cymbeline* was given a straightforward, unfussy production with little extraneous stage business.[8] Indeed for all the modern-dress productions during the twenties, Shelving worked within the original three-stage framework with false proscenium, steps and curtains, established since the earliest days of the theatre. The setting for Philario's house in Rome, a balustrade against a plain background, looks pure Jackson on conception, while the painted decor used for the Welsh scenes, which was typical of Shelving and prefigured those designed for the later productions, consisted of a cut-out frankly stylised cave, flanked by a graceful drooping tree and a distant vista of hills. Actors dressed as footmen or pages drew the grey curtains which separated the upper level from the main stage, sometimes during the progress of a scene. Modern-dress Shakespeare was built on the foundation of methods which had been tried and tested at the Rep for the previous decade.

It was also in keeping with the Rep's general policy that there was little serious bowdlerisation in Ayliff's version of the play and that he cut only some four hundred lines of a very complex text.[9] Ayliff also made an attempt to stage the Vision scene for the first time since the seventeenth century but the fact that the sequence was played in dumb show may have created confusion. Almost certainly the ghosts' speeches were cut because of what was deemed to be stilted archaic verse. When Shakespeare's multiplicity of linguistic styles included apparently primitive verse there was already a critical trend to declare such alleged ineptitude as unShakespearian. In 1928 Ayliff expressed an opinion then current amongst scholars including Granville Barker: '*Cymbeline* is not pure Shakespeare. Whole speeches are not by him. This modern-dress did not do any good. Their rhetorical artificiality seemed to be emphasised by the costume. Yet these made to the genuine Shakespeare passages an extraordinarily firm and lifelike relief. It was as though his characters were of our period'.[9]

The experiment appears to have been a revelation to company and audience alike. As every would-be Shakespearian iconoclast has since discovered, modern-dress productions, especially when staged within a proscenium frame, do not have the neutrality of a simple reading in everyday clothes or even a rehearsal. Every piece of costume necessitates a major decision and makes a statement about each character. A wrist watch, such as Colin Keith-Johnston wore as Hamlet, suddenly becomes a significant accessory. The Rep's tradition of including even the most minor of Shakespeare's characters became an obvious advantage now. Ayliff and Shelving must have derived great satisfaction, not to say fun, in finding appropriate costumes. As Ayliff put it in 1928, characters 'simply sprang into fuller life'. So the audience was delighted to see Cornelius the physician as a smooth Harley Street doctor and the soothsayer as a caricature of a modern spiritualist with 'a black wide-awake hat, a cape, a haggard expression and a long white beard' (*Birmingham Gazette*, 21 April 1923). The gaoler was the hit of the evening: 'Old Bill' from the famous First World War cartoons, with a cockney accent, khaki uniform and red M.P.'s brassard.

Certain scenes deployed ideas which were to be used more elaborately in *Hamlet* and *Macbeth*. The wager scene was played as a leisured discussion while pages carried round trays of cocktails. The final battle was staged in semi-darkness with flashing lights and explosions. Ayliff also learnt from the laughter provoked by Cloten's head wrapped in a decent white cloth which Crompton-Rhodes suggested might have contained 'a hunk of bread and cheese and a few onions' (*Birmingham Post*, 23 April 1923). For *Macbeth* in 1928 'the usurper's cursed head' remained firmly attached to Macbeth's body which was carried in on a bier. Unnecessary laughter was best avoided in view of the unseemly glee with which the press greeted the news of the modern-dress enterprise. Despite protestations by the management that each was an 'experiment', many persisted in calling every modern-dress production a 'stunt'. The catchphrase 'Shakespeare in Plus-Fours' which was to haunt subsequent productions, was adopted when critics realised that Imogen was to set off for Milford Haven in a knicker-bocker suit. Crompton-Rhodes reminded readers of the commercial popularity of Peggy O'Neil, the American comedy actress, whose most recent success *Plus Fours* had been produced at the Savoy Theatre in January 1923.

The sight of Imogen, that most idealised of heroines in the nineteenth-century theatre, dressed in a pink silk jumper and skirt, a knicker-bocker suit and finally a very unflattering blue bersaglieri uniform, brought her down to earth with a bump. Not only was Imogen perceived to be rather an ordinary young woman but Shakespeare himself as a working dramatist, writing within a popular theatrical tradition, came much closer. Wicked stepmothers, jealous husbands, foolish young men, wily villains, plots to poison and the final triumph of virtue were immediately recognised as the stuff of modern melodrama. Characters emerged as traditional types. Cymbeline (Slaine Mills) in a red Field Marshal's uniform complete with VC and DSO, probably benefited when seen as a modern major general and the Queen was an undoubted vamp in her red wig and tight-fitting black gown. Such unsubtle costuming, however, imposed a stereotype on Evelyn Hope who played the Queen. One or two reviews suggest that she became a more credible figure once relieved of the necessity of acting up to the impression created by her first appearance. Bache Matthews recalled that the actors were unnerved by the sheer daring of the enterprise into even more 'fluffing and inaudibility than usual'.[10] Eileen Beldon as Imogen was a particular casualty, although once dressed as a boy she seems to have gained confidence and a stronger voice. Scott Sunderland as Posthumus went into exile in a blue serge lounge suit. For Crompton Rhodes he was 'beautifully English . . . a pleasant gentleman, manly, upright, unsuspecting, and rather thick-headed'.

The actor who gained most was Cedric Hardwicke who played Iachimo. Despite the 'dago' label the performance was for *The Times* critic 'vital, subtle and never for an instant ridiculous' (24 April 1923). Crompton-Rhodes was reminded of Iago 'with a curious sensation of getting closer to Shakespeare's mind than ever before'. Ayliff himself seems to have believed more readily in the character 'I conceived him as an Italian who spoke English perfectly; but I have sometimes wondered if it would not have been better to have given him an Italian accent. My study of the play made me believe that Shakespeare had drawn him from life from an Italian envoy or somebody he knew'.[11] In his autobiography, Cedric Hardwicke claimed that in modern clothes the players 'freed from the trammelling effect of costume seemed to be able to dispense with the grand manner and become more simple and effective'.[12]

The critic of the *Birmingham Evening Despatch* declared that the production had finally shattered the illusions of the bardolaters that Shakespeare was a kind of demi-god, 'incapable . . . of shamelessly writing down to the devotees of melodrama and puppet show' (23 April 1923). Others were inclined to support Crompton Rhodes' view that 'what is good in the play becomes better and what is bad worse'. He found that the bedroom scene and the dirge upon Fidele became 'more real, more convincing . . . and by more real I do not mean less poetic'. The critic of *The Times* agreed: 'The truth of it is that poetry prevails over costume . . . such a lyric as "Fear no more the heat of the sun" suffers nothing from being said by two young men in tweed coats and football shorts'. The review concluded that the production was important '. . . for the lead it gives. A living dramatist who is also a poet, may know now that he can write in verse on modern themes if he can write well enough. It opens a new possibility not to Shakespeare producers but to the contemporary theatre'. But Ayliff was adamant that '*Cymbeline* taught us more than anything else that Shakespeare was a modern author, while its reception proved that there was a public for such productions'.[13] Jackson had been eager to take the production to London. They had either not read or were undeterred by Granville Barker's conclusions on the staging of *Cymbeline* expressed in his first preface to the play published in *The Players Shakespeare* in the autumn of 1923. Meeting all the inconsistencies of the play head on, Granville Barker advocated presenting *Cymbeline* as a masque which emphasised the artificiality of language and character.[14] Also that autumn, in a production of the play which came on tour to the Prince of Wales Theatre in Birmingham, Lewis Casson presented a version which in terms of text and fluid staging aimed to approximate to the original conditions of Shakespeare's day while still providing rich and stimulating settings and costume. However Bruce Winston's dazzling Futurist designs only succeeded in alienating most of the critics.[15] Barker's general remarks on the staging of Shakespeare in the earlier preface to *Macbeth* sounded a note of caution: 'We cannot quite discard the present and . . . entering into the past would be harder still . . . some halfway house of meeting must be found. But let it be insisted that the further we can learn to travel back upon the road the greater profit to us'.[16]

Jackson clearly had no intention of travelling back. Some reviews of *Cymbeline* had suggested that a better play might prove a more appropriate test. A modern-dress *Hamlet* in London was probably not what they had in mind. By August 1925, however, Jackson was in a strong enough position to take on the theatrical establishment. The excitement generated by *Back to Methuselah!*, 1,329 performances of *The Farmer's Wife* at the Court theatre and a knighthood in April 1925 had given him immaculate commercial credentials. The Kingsway theatre, which like the Court was small and intimate, provided another outlet for Birmingham's artistic capital. *Caesar and Cleopatra* inaugurated the new management on 21 April followed by *The New Morality*. Both were directed by Ayliff.

Before the opening night of *Hamlet* at the Kingsway on 25 August 1925, Cedric Hardwicke, who played the First Gravedigger, told the press that 'the production will be the first in which Shakespeare's work has been produced as a play and not as a setting for some star actor' (*Daily News* 30 June 1925). In fact ensemble productions by Bridges-Adams and Robert Atkins as well as J. B. Fagan's 1924 OUDS production, with Gyles Isham as Hamlet, had given the lie to that statement. But it did seem possible to argue that the play was still in the grip of what was left of actor–managers' theatre. Earlier in 1925, in his production mounted at the Haymarket Theatre, the forty-three year old American actor John Barrymore had successfully exploited the traditional notion of a romantic, poetic prince. Despite the power of the central performance and the impressively simple set by Robert Edmond Jones, the text was so heavily cut and Barrymore's interpolated stage business so prolonged, that at least one member of the audience, Gordon Crosse, greeted the final arrival of 'a breezy and robust Fortinbras . . . as a positive relief'.[17]

Colin Keith-Johnston was twenty-eight and had been a member of the Birmingham Repertory Company since 1921. He had played a variety of modern roles including Marchbanks in *Candida*, Oswald in *Ghosts* and Adam and Pygmalion in *Back to Methuselah!* In Shakespeare he had played Benvolio in the 1922 *Romeo and Juliet* and Guiderius in *Cymbeline*. Before *Hamlet* he had spent the previous seventeen months playing a bucolic young lover in *The Farmer's Wife*. He was of slight build, with a modern craggy face — his nose was broken during the war. By his own admission to the *Daily News* he was 'not a success in costume plays'. Gwen

Ffrangçon-Davies has said that Keith-Johnston lacked the appropriate verse-speaking technique which she felt would have been necessary for a more traditional approach to the play. She herself, alarmed by the idea of Shakespeare in short dresses and perhaps afraid she might have to abandon her own technique in the interests of more naturalistic delivery, rejected the role of Ophelia.

In a newsletter article which was circulated before the first performance, Jackson wrote of 'the essential modernity of Shakespeare's characters and the problems of "the man in the street" who comes to see a traditional production'. What Jackson called 'the sublime unnaturalness of blank verse', the strangeness of the costumes and the conventions of Shakespearian acting 'interpose a veil between him and the author's intention and the man in the street comes away with an increased feeling of almost superstitious awe but no understanding that he has been witnessing a real conflict of credible human beings. It is with this end in view that we are producing *Hamlet* just as if it happened today'.[18] Producing *Hamlet* as 'a real conflict of credible human beings' meant preparing the text to give maximum clarity to the unfolding of that conflict. Traditionally the cuts necessary to make the performance of an acceptable length for a modern audience had meant the wholesale eradication of Fortinbras, the Danish and English ambassadors and Rosencrantz and Guildenstern. In focusing all the attention on Hamlet himself, the basic narrative was blurred and the wider social and political context was lost. Ayliff's production which played for just under three hours,[19] provided the audience with the fullest text many would have heard, but sacrificed several famous passages and tended to smooth out the wide range of linguistic styles which is such a marked characteristic of the play. *Hamlet* as a literary text lost much of its philosophical expression of Renaissance culture. As a play for the theatre, the turgid, romantic Victorian monodrama was replaced by a political and psychological thriller.

Horatio's heightened description of the events in Rome before the death of Julius Caesar was missing, as was the lyrical exchange between Marcellus and Horatio which includes 'Some say that ever 'gainst that season comes'. Sadly this meant the loss of Horatio's laconic 'So I have heard and do in part believe it'. Sixteen lines of

105

Claudius's homily to Hamlet on the need to control his grief were cut and nearly all Laertes's sententious advice to Ophelia. He spoke only the seven lines following 'Perhaps he loves you now'. Polonius was only allowed half his rebuke to Ophelia in the same scene and Hamlet lost all but the first four lines of his diatribe against drunkenness and the 'vicious mole of nature'. The Ghost was encouraged to be as brief as possible which meant that some thirty-five lines of his lurid, curiously primitive speeches were by-passed. Perhaps Ayliff was uncomfortable with this manifestation of the supernatural in a modern setting. The Ghost was only heard in the III.iv scene between Hamlet and Gertrude. Indeed in the 1928 *Macbeth* Banquo's ghost was present only in Macbeth's imagination. As several critics pointed out, interest in psychic phenomena was as lively as ever in the twenties, but the ghost in tragedy was felt to be an outmoded theatrical convention.

The political background to the narrative was sketched in succinctly. In the first scene the whole of Horatio's account of the dispute with Norway was cut but it was then Claudius who subsequently gave the information about Fortinbras in his instructions to Cornelius and Voltemand. Later in II.ii Voltemand gave virtually all the report of his successful embassy to Norway. Fortinbras, played by Donald Finlay who doubled as Third Player, did not appear until the end of the play, but his Captain was seen in IV.iv to tell Hamlet of the expedition to gain 'a little patch of land' and thus provoke Hamlet's final soliloquy which was rarely heard in traditional productions. The play ended not with the death of Hamlet, but with the arrival of Fortinbras, the English ambassador's news of the execution of Rosencrantz and Guildenstern and Horatio's abridged explanation of the carnage.

Hamlet's cry 'O good Horatio, I'll take the ghost's word for a thousand pounds' ended the first half of the performance as Claudius escaped from 'The Murder of Gonzago'. Hamlet's subsequent abuse of Rosencrantz and Guildenstern, his taunts over the recorder, the weasel/whale debate with Polonius and finally ''Tis now the very witching time of night' were all cut. Hamlet's scene with Gertrude moved straight into IV.i without a break and the short sequence between Hamlet and his former schoolfellows was also omitted. Claudius's speech at the beginning of IV.iii, 'I have sent to seek him, and to find the body', was inserted after IV.i.39, 'and let them know both what we mean to do'. The accumulative effect was to make the aftermath of Polonius's death move with great speed. Ayliff's basic approach seems to have been to prune back some scenes so that only the bare bones remained. It was most noticeable in IV.vii where about eighty lines of the plot between Laertes and Claudius were cut. Very little was sacrificed to the cause of updating.

For some Ayliff's textual surgery was nothing short of sacrilege. Cedric Hardwicke recalled: 'At one rehearsal an old actor was horror stricken when it was suggested that some famous line would have to go; he walked into a dark corner of the stage, bowed his head and solemnly crossed himself!'.[20] When some critics objected that the play had been reduced to mere melodrama, William Poel wrote to the *Manchester Guardian* to claim that Ayliff had restored *Hamlet* to its original status as a revenge play:

> If then as a piece of literature the full extent is a world famous composition it is equally true that as drama it is faulty because the action is continually being held up to allow of dialogue being spoken which however interesting or entertaining in itself, has no connection with the main story, that of Hamlet's revenge.
>
> (29 August 1925)

As always, speed of action was assisted by the staging. The false proscenium represented two grey stone columns with a built-out ledge at the base of each to form a seat. Two straight stone steps led up to the inner stage. It was, of course, perfectly appropriate for Elsinore to be an ancient stone-built castle still inhabited by a modern royal family. For most full scenes a cloth was hung at the back of the inner stage which depicted an interior wall dominated by two large windows with leaded panes. The prevailing colour was grey. A carpet was laid down the steps and a mock-Victorian gilt chandelier with electric light bulbs hung from the flys. Different coloured curtains on the columns indicated a change of location: green for Laertes's departure for Paris and blue when Ophelia ran 'affrighted' to her father. For the continuous sequence after the interval from III.iii to IV.iv the same full set was used. There was no closet scene as such: the term closet was cut, but a low couch was placed on the main stage below the steps and tapestry curtains were hung down the columns. Hamlet's encounter with the Norwegian captain, Horatio's reading of Hamlet's letter and the plot to kill Hamlet were all played as front scenes before closed curtains. Furniture was kept to a minimum and the director was anxious that the décor should neither overwhelm the play nor appear too modern. Denmark was little more than a vaguely mid-European/ Ruritanian state. Four heavy carved chairs and a table 'of a kind ordinarily seen in castellated strongholds' (*Evening Standard*, 22 August 1925), were used in various arrangements on the upper stage. Polonius sat at a desk while he questioned Ophelia about Hamlet's love. Critics liked the way the self-important father busily wrote a letter while he issued his heartbreaking instructions to his daughter.

The prompt-book tells us that the actors on the stage laughed and probably the audience with them, as Polonius advised Laertes that 'the apparel oft proclaims the man'. 'Proclaiming the man' was achieved with great care, revealing people of flesh and blood in characters formerly smothered by their ornate costumes. Polonius (A. Bromley-Davenport) usually played as a tedious old clown, emerged as a dapper elder statesman first seen in white tie and tails. For his farewell to his son, he wore a formal dark three piece suit, winged collar and bow tie as he eyed his son's casual light tweed suiting. Later in morning coat, striped trousers and spats he fumbled with a pince-nez as he struggled to read Hamlet's love letter. To the critic of the *Liverpool Weekly Post* he looked 'like the elderly and worldly wise French count of musical comedy' (29 August 1925), especially when he ogled the girls in the players' company. Ophelia was not, as some newspapers reported, an ultra-modern flapper which might have made her submission to her father seem rather improbable. The intention was to emphasise her extreme youth and inexperience; indeed Muriel Hewitt celebrated her eighteenth birthday during the run of the production. Alan Bland, Jackson's publicity manager, explained 'Ophelia is just a girl fresh from school with a fussy father and a prig of a brother and a dress suitable to such a young person will be thought out.'[6] (*Evening News*, 22 July 1925.) Muriel Hewitt's hair was not shingled but remained long, plaited and wound into 'winkles' round her ears. She wore a plain cream satin frock which reached to just below her knees and 'nude' stockings. For the play scene she was dressed debutante-style, in foxglove pink.

That there is so much detailed information about the costuming is due to the immense publicity which extended as far as the fashion magazines. Ayliff wanted Gertrude (Dorothy Massingham) to be smartly, but not too fashionably dressed. Even so her shingled red-gold hair excited much comment. After the first night Crompton Rhodes wrote of 'a woman who is afraid that youth is slipping from her' (*Birmingham Daily Post*, 26 August 1925). *The Sketch* (2 September 1925) described her as 'suave, an amoureuse, terribly embarrassed, yet always a great lady'. *The Westminster Gazette* (23 September 1925) gave details of a sea-green frock with 'slanting flounces deepening to an almost emerald shade'. To greet Rosencrantz and Guildenstern she wore a short tight-skirted red lace 'afternoon dress' and for the play scene was resplendent in gold tissue with a square train, a gold head-dress, an orange chiffon scarf and a huge orange feather fan. A full-length dark orange negligée was considered appropriate for her traumatic interview with her son.

It must be obvious then, that modern dress provided ample opportunity for Shelving to indulge his love of period costume even though the period was of the present day. The ladies' dresses and hats were specially made by a London couturier and each actor had as many, if not more, costumes as in a traditional production. It says a good deal for Ayliff's skill that once the initial shock was over, nothing seemed frivolous or inappropriate. Actors benefited from the ease and naturalness of well-fitting modern clothes 'attained to the dignity of a skin'.

The first sight of Claudius was of a sophisticated man, elegant in tailed evening dress with a pale blue garter ribbon across his chest. Later he wore a black morning coat and waistcoat, dark striped trousers, winged collar and broad cravat and sported a button hole. For the *Tailor and Cutter*, this ensemble proved too much: 'The King's crimes were forgotten and he suggested the paddock at Ascot'.[21] Frank Vosper, who played Claudius, wrote about the experience in the October edition of *Theatre World*. He described the momentary panic he felt on his first entrance:

I long to feel the reassurance of robes about me, to know that even if I am looking pompous and theatrical at any rate I am decorative. As it is I have nothing to fall back on . . . [But] I am conscious that Claudius has benefited perhaps more than any other character by the clothes of today . . . I play him clean shaven, silver haired at the temples and — I hope — fairly soigné; in fact sufficiently attractive to account for Gertrude's frailty and 'o'er hasty marriage'.

Ironically, when provided with some semblance of traditional costuming — a mauve dressing gown to cover his trousers for his prayer scene — his polished naturalism seems to have deserted him. The setting was an uneasy mixture of the old and new. A prie-dieu was placed before a gold curtain on the upper rostrum, but before Claudius sought spiritual consolation, he calmed himself after the shock of the play with a whisky and soda poured from the decanter and soda siphon set out on a table positioned on the main stage. Despite what his article calls 'the inspiring hiss' of the soda siphon, Vosper clearly found it difficult to speak the emotional high-flown language of his soliloquy in a restrained manner. George Sampson in the *Weekly Westminster* stated that Vosper while 'perfect as the modern king, was ludicrously ineffective when he tried the barnstorming manner, and he missed a splendid opportunity of showing how a difficult scene should be played' (2 September 1925). After Claudius had despatched Hamlet to England, a small piece of business was introduced that might have some straight from a modern thriller. As the curtain drew across, the King moved away and then shrank back at the sight of Polonius's blood. He bent down to touch the spot with his finger.

Vosper's account highlights the extent to which traditional costume not only obscured the character, but also protected the actor. The task of making Claudius credible in modern dress became the much more fundamental task of making Claudius himself credible. In a lengthy and illuminating essay in the *Fortnightly Review*, John Palmer suggested that in the traditional production the monstrous Claudius is presented entirely from his nephew's point of view. Vosper's Claudius was a much more complex character:

Superficially the more agreeable fellow. Almost certainly he did not, like his predecessor sleep within his orchard every afternoon . . . The audience instead of merely waiting for Claudius to be killed . . . is interested in a real duel between the two men. This not only makes the play interesting as a play; it makes Hamlet's own motives and conduct more intelligible. Take for example, the famous irresolution with which he so often taxes himself. This irresolution is in the conventional Hamlet quite incomprehensible. No one would hesitate five minutes about killing the conventional horrid monster of the romantic stage . . . It is quite another matter to make away with the pleasant gentleman presented by Mr Vosper.[22]

Other characters emerged from the total anonymity imposed by past productions. Ayliff's treatment of the text removed most of the justification for Hamlet's description of Rosencrantz and Guildenstern as 'adders fanged'. Dressed in fashionable double-breasted tweed suits, they were simply young men, fellow students, greeted initially with great joy by Hamlet. The critic of the *Weekly Scotsman* (5 September 1925) found their motives quite plain when viewed 'as a couple of ordinary undergraduates overcome by the honour of being invited to Court'. The *Daily Mirror* (26 August 1925) commented that in their presence: 'Hamlet's philosophising gained the appropriate undergraduate quality which made those utterances about shadows and dreams and "the paragon of animals" understandable as the thoughts of a very young man and not the pretentious mouthings of an actor–manager'.

Both Horatio (Alan Howland) and Laertes (Robert Holmes), though played by two virtually unknown actors, gained enormously. The tragedy of Laertes became much more obvious. He was seen as a pleasant up-to-date young man giving advice to Ophelia while addressing a luggage label to Paris, and finally kissing her affectionately. He returned, as Hubert Griffiths put it, 'warped by a rancorous hatred in his heart' (*Daily Chronicle*, 1 September 1925). The techniques drawn from modern naturalistic acting helped to define character. Horatio kept his hands in the pockets of his brown lounge suit while he imparted the incredible news about the ghost. Gordon Crosse notice that he paused on 'I saw him — once' as though momentarily wary of saying 'yesternight' too soon.[23] Despite the loss of a substantial number of lines, it was reported by the critic of the *Sheffield Mail* (3 September 1925) that Howland 'by

111

his attitude even more than by his words shows that the friendship between the two is more than the cordial relationship of prince and courtier'.

John Shand in the *New Statesman* (5 September 1925) accused Jackson and Ayliff of changing Hamlet, 'the witty, melancholy, thoughtful and imaginative Prince of Denmark into Horatio, the honest, the middle-class, the mediocre'. Shand wanted a 'superman'. What he got was a young man in a lounge suit with a black crêpe band arounds his arm. 'Always' as Hubert Griffiths remarked 'slightly and subtly worse dressed than the Court'. When he teased Polonius, Hamlet pulled out the bow in the older man's natty dress tie. After the murder of Polonius, Hamlet, with his tie dangling and in shirt sleeves and braces, confronted an immaculate Claudius. The poetic prince was completely absent. Critics noticed Colin Keith-Johnston's staccato delivery and his disconcertingly limited breath control in the long speeches. But Edith Shackleton in the *Evening Standard* (26 August 1925), praised his 'gift of getting out even the most subtle speeches, as though they had but instantly come into his head'. He was 'cubbish . . . fiery and farouche' (*Manchester Guardian* 26 August 1925), pointed out that 'Shakespeare's Hamlet is something very different from a good-looking elocutionist . . . he is loose tongued, bawdy minded and savage product of youthful disenchantment'. Hamlet's insult 'A little more than kin and less than kind' was blurted out in Claudius's face, and not as the usual aside. The cruelty and ugliness of this interpretation made complete sense of Hamlet's abuse of his mother and step-father which was otherwise reduced, in Brown's view, 'to preposterous rubbish' in a traditional production.

The opening scene was played in semi-darkness. It was just possible to see Barnardo and Francisco meet on the main stage dressed in heavy military great coats with Danish service caps and carrying rifles with fixed bayonets. The ghost, played by Shelving's brother Grosvenor North, appeared on the steps in front of a cloth painted with the outline of battlements and the suggestion of cannon. After much discussion, it was decided that the ghost should wear the uniform of a Danish general with an enormous military cloak and peaked hat. Horatio's reference to the 'beaver' of his helmet was cut. With the costume fabric treated to give off a faint luminous sheen, he looked, in the words of *The Spectator*, like 'a faintly silvered father Christmas' (5 September 1925). When the battlement curtain was drawn back and the lights blazed for the entrance of the Danish Court, there was apparently an audible gasp from the audience. The prompt-book is vague on exactly how the entry was presented but the press reviews were eloquent on their sense of shock. Ann Temple, the drama critic of the *Glasgow Bulletin*, described the scene:

> Courtiers in "swallow-tails"; the Queen in a short dress with a fish tail train, monocled men and smoking women, footmen in plush and a short stout lady in magenta velvet and diamond tiara . . . Hamlet, a moody boyish figure in the foreground with a dark lounge suit and soft collar, dejection in every line of his hunched shoulders and sprawling feet. What effects Mr Keith-Johnston achieved throughout the evening with just that little turn inward of his right foot (26 August 1925).

A marked feature of the production was the absence of lengthy ceremonial entrances. Ayliff seems to have concentrated on evoking the atmosphere of a leisured royal household in the midst of which the emotional and psychological drama was played out. Claudius, smoking a cigarette, moved slowly to the rostrum, bowing to his courtiers and giving a special welcome to his ambassadors. The Queen, however, went straight to talk to her son. Vosper described in his article how he concealed his annoyance with a diplomatic smile, before beckoning to Gertrude to join him. Cocktails were served and an unseen orchestra played syncopated dance music. When the royal party left the stage, a grey curtain was drawn across so that Hamlet came through the central opening to speak his first soliloquy and meet Horatio. The strains of the Charleston could be heard in the background.

When Rosencrantz and Guildenstern arrived at court they found the Queen, the court chaplain and two other courtiers playing bridge at a table set at an angle by the right window. Other courtiers stood around chatting while a footman carried a tray of coffee cups. As Gertrude rose to greet the visitors, the bridge party exited and footmen cleared and rearranged the table and all but one of the chairs up against the window where they remained until the play scene. After Gertrude had expressed her feelings about Hamlet's madness, 'I doubt it is no other but the main/His father's death and our o'er hasty marriage', she clearly felt the need to reassure her new husband. As he turned away, she followed him, touched him on the shoulder and they embraced. While Claudius talked to Voltemand, she walked upstage to the chair and sat with her back half-turned to the audience.

Anne Temple and other critics noticed how the naturalistic techniques taken from the performance of modern plays invested familiar passages with new significance. Even before the first night, Dorothy Massingham pointed out the similarity between Gertrude's scene with Hamlet and the final scene of Noel Coward's controversial play *The Vortex* (A. Bromley-Davenport had played in the 1924 cast). After the interview with her son in Ayliff's production, Gertrude threw herself sobbing on to the couch but rose and shrank away from Claudius when he attempted to touch her. She evaded him again on 'What, Gertrude? How does Hamlet?' and went back to sit on the couch. After Rosencrantz and Guildenstern had been despatched to find Hamlet, she exited slowly while Claudius sat down and lit a cigarette.

The *Sketch* critic wrote of Hamlet's scene with Ophelia that Keith-Johnston used his tongue 'as a club' on the girl. She sat reading on the rostrum while he hammered out 'To be or not to be' striding restlessly up and down the stage. On seeing Ophelia, he went up the steps to put his hands on the back of the chair, turning away when she rose and unclasped the necklace he had given her. On 'Go, farewell, or if thou wilt needs marry', he came down the steps and went to drag her down with him. Finally he put his arms round her and then left her collapsed and crying. Anne Temple commented:

> The soliloquy that may be relished in the text by the fireside always rouses an imp of doubt, elocuted as even the best Shakespearean actors seem impelled to speak it, hindered, it may be by their archaic garments from the natural restlessness or ruminative stillness in which tense thought is generally clothed today. "To be or not to be" gains a new naturalness from a hands-in-pocket restless pacing; and that — to actresses most trying because most stilted — speech "Oh what a noble mind is here o'erthrown" seemed almost credible whimpered to a chair-back by a broken hearted flapper.

114

What a review in the November edition of the *Midlander* called the 'Pirandellian confusion of the play scene', became visually the high point of the evening. The arrival of the ultra-smart actors drew an appreciative laugh from the audience. The First Player (Terence O'Brien), wore glowing chestnut-coloured 'plus fives' with vivid golfing socks and carried an ebony cane which he used to great effect while delivering Aeneas' tale to Dido. Another player sported a lavish astrakhan-collared coat while the actresses displayed the latest autumn fashions — the 'altitude of a chopine' could still be an appropriate reference to their high-heeled shoes. Hamlet gave his instructions to the actors in front of a grey curtain while the orchestra was heard tuning up behind the scenes. Crompton Rhodes remarked that 'The Murder of Gonzago' was presented rather like a Victorian command performance at Windsor Castle. As the curtains were drawn back, the Fourth Player (Charles Leighton) was seen directing the footmen to arrange the seating. Claudius and Gertrude entered to the strains of the Danish national anthem and then sat, with their backs to the audience, stage centre on a low settee facing the rostrum. The upper stage was now set to look like a portable 'fit-up' with its own footlights and a quaint pictorial drop curtain. Members of the court sat on benches on either side of the King and Queen and a footman carried sateen-covered programmes on a tray. The play itself became a parody of a traditional production with the actors dressed in elaborate medieval robes and using extravagant elocution and gesture, before a back-cloth painted in true Joseph Harker pictorial fashion. The dumb show and the greater part of the Player King's long speech were cut. A piano accompanied the action with what the prompt-book terms 'sleep music' and the lights flickered luridly when Lucianus entered. Tradition was abruptly shattered when the modern prince Hamlet exuberantly kicked up his legs at the success of his plan. The *Weekly Scotsman* recalled 'vividly the king and queen in sharp black silhouette against the brightly coloured scene . . . so that a tense movement of their hands dominates all'.

As might be expected the press commented on the ingenious devices employed to evade problems posed by the text. The sword with which Hamlet threatened the praying Claudius and later killed Polonius was taken from one of the two decorative suits of armour placed on either side of the stage. There was some amusement when Laertes threatened the King with what looked like a modern six-shooter. They may have also noticed that when Hamlet asked Gertrude to 'Look here upon this picture and on this' he indicated the traditional picture locket around her neck but then drew from his pocket a photograph of her first husband. Cigarettes, as we have seen, proved invaluable hand props. Gordon Crosse recorded that when Hamlet said 'I humbly thank you sir' to the Norwegian captain he was accepting a cigarette which he then smoked through 'How all occasions do inform against me'. More fundamentally the extra business appears to have enhanced the imaginative and emotional response of the audience. The critic of the October edition of *Vogue* wrote: 'King, Queen and courtiers stopped being clothes props to become suffering human beings like ourselves. The scene in the palace while the mob howl outside for Laertes, and the King and Queen shiver for their lives amid breaking glass was very moving in its modernity.'

Opinion was divided about Muriel Hewitt's Ophelia. Some supported the view of the *Daily News*: 'pretty and dutiful to her father as a very young flapper in Surbiton who didn't go to nightclubs might be, and really upset and bewildered by this Hamlet business' (26 August 1925). But the review in the *Queen* (2 September 1925) spoke of her integrity in the mad scenes as 'immeasurably more moving than the conventional floral posturing'. She went mad, not in white satin, but in a short flimsy black frock. The fact that she sang all the lines of her bawdy songs — to their traditional tunes but offset by a few modern dance steps — revealed the element of sexual repression and several reviews commented on the newly fashionable Freudian dimension. Her flowers were woven into a wreath round her hair and she carried others which she dropped on seeing Claudius in the second sequence. She placed rosemary in Laertes's hand, a pansy in his button hole and then threw the fennel and columbine at the King. As she sang 'And will a not come again', she sat on the steps picking up the flowers and making them into a posy.

Her funeral took place in a very modern atmosphere of refined vulgarity; 'Kensal Green with floral tributes' as Edith Shackleton put it. The grave was represented as a plain rectangular stone vault resting on the steps. The upper stage was dominated by a huge unadorned cross set centrally on a triple-layered plinth. Shelving's back-cloth, which had probably been used, dimly lit, for Hamlet's encounter with the ghost, was eerily expressionistic, depicting the pale shapes of crowded tombstones. An obelisk loomed on one side and on the other Shelving painted a marble angel with curving wings and folded arms. The pall-draped coffin was borne by soldiers and the court chaplain now wore a biretta and a white lace surplice. Cedric Hardwicke was fully aware of the break with tradition in his own performance. In his autobiography he described the comic turn of the traditional grave digger: adlibbing, peeling off endless layers of waistcoats as well as performing a spade dance.[24] Hardwicke had scored a considerable success as the Devonian Churdles Ash in *The Farmer's Wife*. Now he was a cockney labourer in a rusty Sunday-best suit and bowler, with red-spotted handkerchief sticking out of his trousers. His mate (H. M. Bradford) wore corduroys tied at the knee. The huddled group of silent mourners, the depressingly familiar details of ropes and webbing to lower the coffin and the wreaths which Hardwicke helped arrange, evoked a realistically funereal atmosphere. When Hamlet bellowed out 'I loved Ophelia' and fought with Laertes in the grave, it was a genuinely shocking moment. After Hamlet had withdrawn from the stage, the King came down to speak to Laertes who was subsequently left alone for a moment until black velvet curtains were drawn across.

Osric arrived dressed in extravagant Oxford bags, a short blue 'reefer' jacket and carrying a trilby hat. Speaking in a fluting, high-pitched voice he proved to be an entertaining diversion, although Ayliff cut most of Hamlet's satirical commentary. The preparations for the duel were deceptively relaxed and there was no formal entrance. The King and Laertes emerged together while servants including Osric, Marcellus and Barnardo carried on fencing foils and organised the set. The match was judged from the vantage point of a low cushioned settee placed below the steps. Hamlet was still dressed in his notorious tweed plus-fours from the graveyard scene, while Laertes wore a cable-knit cardigan over his flannel trousers. Gertrude and the other courtiers did not arrive until after Hamlet selected his foil and made his apology to Laertes. The inevitable footman carried round a tray of drinks. The line 'this pearl is thine' was cut. Claudius simply poured poison into the glass which Gertrude drank from. She died slumped in her chair while the wounded Laertes was helped to the side of the stage. As Hamlet advanced on Claudius, the King retreated to a table on the upper stage where Hamlet stabbed him with a foil — he did not force the drink on the King. Osric and another servant dragged Hamlet away to collapse on the settee as Claudius staggered down the steps and then up again to die at Gertrude's feet. The Chaplain knelt beside the body. The final effect of the stage littered with corpses was as disconcerting as usual, perhaps more so. For the critic of the *Sheffield Mail* the scene took on the lurid quality of a modern melodrama: 'Lying on the stage are four dead bodies, one in a sweater and flannel bags. Another in a sports suit with plus-fours, a third in gent's best suiting and the last in what I believe is known to the initiated as an afternoon tea-gown. It is too much'. He did, however, acknowledge that the fault might lie with Shakespeare rather than Ayliff.

There were many well known faces in the first-night audience, including Ben Greet, Godfrey Tearle, Frank Benson and Jackson's theatrical 'godfather', William Poel. The following day Poel wrote a letter which remains in Jackson's personal archive:

> Your achievement is another nail in the coffin of the rotten traditions associated with the acting of *Hamlet* on the stage which came into vogue in the time of Betterton. I don't think that a nearer approach to an Elizabethan rendering of the play on the stage has before been reached by a producer. The notable features to me were, (1) the even cast with no intrusion of the "star" tradition: (2) The retention of Hamlet's lines following after the closet scene, including that most illuminating soliloquy "How all occasions do inform against me" etc.: (3) The recognition of the King and Queen as prominent characters in the play, not only because they are a King & a Queen but that they also are the pivot of the plot: (4) The realistic and natural — that is non-theatrical — staging of the Ophelia scenes, especially noticeable at the grave.
>
> I was not impressed, however, by the handling of the play-scene. I have always contended that Hamlet would be the last person to wish the mimic play to end where it does. He wants the court to see the representation of the second marriage given by the play-actors. In fact he says so. I take it he is speaking to the Court — *not* to the King

when he exclaims "You shall see [anon] how the murtherer gets the love of Gonzago's wife". But the King again defeats Hamlet's intention by stopping the performance at the critical moment. There's no confusion! The crisis of the scene does not come until Hamlet's tussle with Ros: and Guild: which follows directly afterwards. This dialogue should be given with much anger and passion by the three speakers.

The whole performance, though, is a record in our stage-history of the play. The *Hamlet* of the Betterton and Kemble school I hope may never again be seen in our theatre.[25]

If Poel looked back to the Elizabethans, others found the value of the production lay in its revelation of the timelessness of Shakespeare's play: that it was possible to make Shakespeare accessible to the modern world. John Palmer reminded his readers that many young playgoers had now been brought 'more directly into contact with Shakespeare's original play . . . Shakespeare would gain enormously if each generation could read his plays for itself finding in them what it required for its own purposes and its own inspiration'. When Peter Hall presented David Warner's young unconventional Hamlet in 1965 he stated that the play 'turns a new face to each century, even to each decade. It is a mirror which gives back the reflection of the age that is contemplating it'.[26] Forty years before, Ivor Brown wrote that Colin Keith-Johnston's performance,

With its gabbling cynical world hatred and its mood of relentless raillery was a perfect expression of a shell-shocked age . . . it is the right diet and medicine for an age of heart-break houses and it is wasted upon a time of sleek and smiling security. This was the first heart-break Hamlet I have seen and the best.

Chapter Seven
Modern-Dress Shakespeare: 1927–1929

It is now possible to see that the Rep's modern-dress experiments initiated a profound shift in Shakespearian production values, but it took time to effect the conceptual change which has led us in the late twentieth century to seek automatically for present-day relevance in classical texts. To many of Jackson's contemporaries, including Bridges-Adams and Granville Barker, modern dress was little more than window dressing. But as *Hamlet* brought Jackson and Ayliff an international reputation so the idea was rapidly taken up outside Britain. The Rep production, with the same cast, ran in Birmingham for three weeks from 9 November 1925, just as Horace Brisbin Liveright's modern-dress *Hamlet* opened in New York at the Booth Theatre. Ayliff himself was then invited to direct the play in Vienna with Reinhardt's Hamlet, Alexander Moissi, as the Prince. It is ironic, then, that the third modern-dress experiment was almost ignored. *All's Well that Ends Well* had its first night in Birmingham on Saturday 16 April 1927 and ran for two weeks. It was only the fifth professional production of the play in the twentieth century. Birmingham received the advance publicity with little excitement and it had none of the glamour associated with the London productions. There were few reviews and theatre historians have paid it scant attention. The production's main claim to fame, with hindsight, was the success of the nineteen year old Laurence Olivier as Parolles.[1]

It could be said that *All's Well that Ends Well*, along with its fellow so-called 'problem plays', belongs to the twentieth century and has responded most happily to updating. For Shaw, writing in the 1890s, it was the question of moral ambiguity which was the attraction.

120

Shaw's perception that Shakespeare was exploring the intellectual problem of human inconsistency in *All's Well* led him to make a direct comparison with the work of Ibsen and especially *A Doll's House*. Although Ibsen's plays helped to inaugurate the age of modern prose drama, by the 1920s they were regarded by some as period pieces. The Rep produced *An Enemy of the People* in modern dress in the autumn of 1926 and staged *A Doll's House* for the first time a few months after *All's Well*.

When William Poel directed *All's Well* in 1920, he wanted to reveal continuities in the play between the issue of class differences within marriage in the sixteenth century and the twentieth-century debate about female emancipation. Robert Speaight records a gesture towards modern dress in a rehearsal demand for the King of France to be presented onstage in a bath-chair wheeled by a nurse in V.A.D. uniform.[2] Two of the most successful productions after the Second World War, Tyrone Guthrie's in 1959 and Trevor Nunn's in 1981, both set the play in the early years of this century. Guthrie went still further and derived most of the comedy of the Italian scenes from memories of the Second World War. In 1927 Ayliff's relatively modest production anticipated much of his successors' work.

Shaw was present on the first night. Perhaps it is not too whimsical to suggest that the production of the play he described as 'rooted in my deeper affections' was a Shavian command performance. At least two reviews drew an analogy with *Man and Superman*, asserting that Helena in her vigorous pursuit of her chosen man was a prototype for Ann Whitfield. Crompton Rhodes described Eileen Beldon's Helena as 'a modern, determined, charming, Eton-cropped young woman with a nice taste in frocks' (*Birmingham Daily Post*, 18 April 1927). Indeed similar comparisons with Shaw's New Woman were made in 1959 and 1981. Although it may be critically useful, however, to propose that updating supplies a Shavian gloss to a Shakespearian theme, it is doubtful that Shaw himself saw 'the sovereign charm of the young Helen' in quite that light. Even what little we know of Eileen Beldon's performance hints at a rather more deeply-felt characterisation. In 1895 Shaw stated that the part of Helena was 'still too genuine and beautiful and modern for the public'.[3]

121

Unlike *Hamlet*, *All's Well* was not associated with any well-established theatrical traditions and there was no tried and tested version of the text. Robert Atkins's 1921 Old Vic production had done much to restore the original text, especially the 'indelicate' passages, and attempted to emphasise the play's comedy. In 1922 for the Stratford Festival, Bridges-Adams produced what T. C. Kemp later termed a 'pleasant performance'[4] which implies a degree of bowdlerisation. However Baliol Holloway earned praise for his swaggering Parolles, unlike Ernest Milton in Atkins' production, who seems to have been embarrassed and undermined by the restored text. Ayliff's production ran true to form. The text was cut briskly but carefully with the loss of just four hundred lines. The play was staged in the familiar manner with three main back-cloths and a variety of front curtains to signal the constant switching of location. The King of France's first appearance in front of a blue curtain was played as if in an ante-room in the palace while the Countess despatched Lavache to court in what the prompt-book terms 'a corridor' at Rousillon indicated by a red curtain.

The play was not seriously expurgated but the sexual content of some sequences was discreetly pruned. In the virginity debate between Parolles and Helena in 1.i, Parolles's basic argument that 'It is not politic in the commonwealth of nature to preserve virginity,' was retained but 'underminers and blowers-up' and Parolles' various picturesque images of the state of virginity (cheese which 'consumes itself to the very paring', dates and porridge and 'our French wither'd pear'), were omitted. Helena's last contribution to the discussion was the question 'How might one do, sir, to lose it to her own liking?'. She also lost most of what Shaw called her 'rapturous outburst' in the eleven lines of her speech beginning 'Not my virginity yet./There shall your master have a thousand loves'. On the other hand the 'foul-mouth'd and calumnious knave' Lavache, who had proved very entertaining in Nugent Monck's 1924 amateur Maddermarket production, now lost only thirty lines of his curious blend of obscenity and homily. In 1959 Guthrie could find no place for him at all.

After his enforced marriage, Bertram simply declared his intention to go to the Tuscan wars, omitting the threat 'and never bed her'. But his letter to Helena was given in full, as was Helena's bargain with the Florentine widow. Virtually all of Bertram's wooing of Diana and the substance of the Dumaine Brothers' comments on his behaviour were included. The story of the bed trick was made quite clear. The only noticeably heavy cutting came in the final scene where Ayliff seems to have been anxious to speed towards the dénouement by avoiding the convolutions of Diana's riddling accusations. Bertram's lie that Diana had thrown the King's ring from 'a casement' was considered unnecessary and most of the references to the couple in bed together were cut. The rhythmic, incantatory quality of the verse in Diana's final speech was sacrificed to a more matter of fact introduction to the apparent miracle. She simply said:

> Good mother, fetch my bail. Stay, royal sir;
> The jeweller that owes the ring is sent for,
> And he shall surety me . . .
> . . . one that's dead is quick—
> And now behold the meaning.

In general Ayliff rejected a lot of the gnomic rhyming verse of the play, especially that associated with Helena. The quasi-mystical dimension to the King's cure in II.i was largely bypassed. Ayliff cut 135-139 beginning 'He that of greatest works is finisher' and then 147-151 and 160-163, which includes 'Inspired merit so by breath is barr'd' and 'Ere twice the horses of the sun shall bring'. Helena did not express her willingness to face 'Tax of impudence,/A strumpet's boldness, a divulged shame'. The King did not speak his wondering 'Methinks in thee some blessed spirit doth speak'. It must be remembered that the play was produced against a background of scholarly contempt for the language of *All's Well* which, according to John Dover Wilson in 1929 'would seem to belong to a Shakespeare at his most immature and inept'.[5] The removal of the despised verse would make naturalistic speaking much easier and would intend to encourage a view of Helena as a more prosaic, down-to-earth doctor's daughter.

The drama critic of the *Manchester Guardian* (22 April 1927), however, reviewed the production as if *All's Well* were a brand new comedy written in verse 'following the dangerous example of Mr Ashley Dukes'. The review claimed that Ayliff's production had deliberately set out to subvert Shakespere's verse rhythms 'by combining the modern actor's vice of mumbling and slurring the words with an ingenious breaking up of the lines into jerky prose'. Shakespeare's play, the critic decided, more than equalled the Noel Coward/Frederick Lonsdale treatment of sexual problems. In terms of plot construction 'his comedy has enough incident in it to furnish dozens of "spring cleanings" and "fallen angels" '[6] in sharp contrast to the almost plotless conversational pieces of the modern dramatists. Scrambling Shakespeare's verse, the critic objected, could mean obscuring the intricacies of the story. But setting aside this complaint, the review was one of several which found that the production illuminated Shakespeare's comic skill. There is little information about Ayliff's injection of comic business, but some reviews suggested parallels with modern farce which must have pleased the director. Ben Travers, whose *A Cuckoo in the Nest* inaugurated the 'Aldwych farces' in 1925, was not mentioned but there were references to Pinero whose farces written in the 1880s and 90s had been very popular. In 1928 Ayliff may have been thinking of Feydeau (*The Girl from Maxim's* was seen in London in 1902) when he stated that *All's Well* could be seen in a modern framework as 'a typically French play', even suggesting that Shakespeare had derived the play from a French source.[7] Indeed Ayliff and Shelving focused on the French setting to establish the tone of the production. In 'Producing the Comedies', Jackson recalled: '*All's Well* opened in a delightfully French atmosphere with the Countess swathed in the crêpe so beloved of Gallic widows and Helena in a very simple dress to indicate her position as a dependent'. The emphasis on speed meant that words were often unintelligible and new scenes began before the actors from the previous scene had left the stage. Crompton Rhodes acknowledged this. But with the experience of five other productions of *All's Well* behind him, he declared that a previously difficult story had become 'as plain as a pike-staff' in modern dress.

The play began on the terrace of the chateau of Rousillon. Shelving's back-cloth incorporated imposing practicable double doors placed centrally and surrounded by windows shaded by jaunty striped awnings. The simple wicker garden furniture on stage for the first scene was augmented at the end of the play with cut-out urns of painted flowers.[8] Any sense of gloom suggested by Margaret Chatwin's Countess in her full-length black veil would have been dispelled by gay colours. The first scene took place amidst the bustle and excitement of Bertram's departure. The steward, Rinaldo, opened the double doors to admit a singing valet and a maid both carrying luggage. As they exited Helena came in and went upstage left while the steward stood beside the door as the Countess, Lafeu and Bertram entered. Throughout the conversation with his elders, Bertram was busy with his valet, putting on his coat as he asked about the King's illness, and clearly taking no notice of Helena. She picked up the Countess's dropped scarf, giving the Countess an opportunity to take her arm on 'This young gentlewoman had a father'. Helena seems to have broken free as Lafeu joined in the praise of the dead physician, and then retreated further away left as the farewells to Bertram drew to an end. He crossed to shake her hand on 'Be comfortable to my mother' before exiting with his valet. Helena was left alone to speak her soliloquy, but only after the steward had peeped through the door to observe her, before he too disappeared.

Helena flopped into a chair on 'there is no living, none,/If Bertam be away', only to get up on 'But now he's gone'. She heard Parolles offstage but his entry was delayed while she peered through the door and then introduced him to the audience before returning to her chair. He arrived laden down with coat, stick, gloves and scarf. Their debate on the virgin state concluded, Parolles was more concerned with his coat than her half-abstracted 'Now shall he—/I know not what he shall.'. He merely grunted 'Eh?' in response. He then managed to drop all his possessions and so their farewells were complicated by the business of picking them up as he talked. Helena helped him on with his coat and they both laughed as he turned back to advise her to 'Get thee a good husband'. He did not, in 1927, promise to 'return perfect courtier'.

When the action returned from Paris to the terrace at Rousillon, the Countess was discovered sitting sewing while she talked with her steward. Lavache, named in the programme as a manservant to the Countess, was heard humming offstage. He sang all the lines of his songs, sniggering at the steward as he joked about the needs of the flesh. The *Birmingham Gazette* (18 April 1927) considered the modernisation of the domestic role of Lavache one of the most valuable aspects of the production. 'The clown is by common consent the least funny of Shakespeare's fools . . . But given a feather duster instead of a coxcomb and a black apron instead of motley, and add the incalculable aid of Mr William Pringle's funniest facial antics and this barren humorist is translated into a facetious impudent manservant, and, as such, irresistibly funny'. Perhaps taking a hint from Parolles's description of Lavache in II.iv, 'A good knave, i'faith, and well fed', the little scene where the Countess despatches Lavache to court, was played with the servant snatching grapes from her hand during the 'O Lord, sir!' pantomime.

Helena's choice of her husband took place in the same simple 'room in the palace' where earlier the King had delivered his farewell advice to the young French soldiers. Helena sat centre-stage with the King on her left while Lafeu brought on four Lords who stood downstage right between him and Bertram. The sequence which, years later, Guthrie and Nunn turned into a dance, was choreographed by Ayliff as a neat routine. Directed by Lafeu, each young man bowed first to the King and then moved up to Helena before going stage right as he was rejected. The four finished up standing in a square while Bertram and the King stood either side of Helena. There is no record in the prompt-book of how Bertram registered his rejection of Helena beyond an instruction for Bertram to turn away from the King on 'I cannot love her, nor will strive to do't'. But it is made clear how the reconciliation at the end of the play was anticipated. In II.v, when Bertram ordered Helena home, she went to leave and then turned on 'Pray, sir, your pardon' to request a farewell kiss from her new husband. Bertram started towards her only to stop on hearing Parolles chuckle. As Helena, rather than Bertram, said 'Farewell', she crossed to the left while Parolles, laughing again, moved right. Bertram, obviously registering mixed emotions, looked after her as she left the stage. The *Evening Despatch* (18 April 1927) objected that in 1927, a shingled, short-skirted bride would never be so submissive. The first half of the performance ended with a defiant Bertram rejoining Parolles and exiting stage right.

Parolles can be played as a sort of irresponsible father-figure to

Bertram but Olivier's Parolles was a very young man: a chuckling, corrupting presence. Both the *Evening Despatch* and the *Birmingham Gazette* praised the subtlety of his performance. The *Despatch* was reminded of Iago 'yet never sinister enough to be taken seriously'. Crompton Rhodes found the key to the character in Lafeu's comment 'there can be no kernel in this light nut; the soul of this man is in his clothes'. Rhodes felt that Olivier had indeed made him 'an empty kernel — a real nut in the sense of 1914, well dressed, good-looking, pleasant mannered'. For the sake of modern dress, Ayliff cut the references to Parolles's 'scarfs and bannerets' but when Lafeu insulted the young man with 'who's his tailor?' he peered at the label on the back of his collar.

In the second half of the play, the emphasis was very much on comedy. The young men now wore military uniform and the colours of the modern French military forces would have proved a real asset here. The ordinary soldiers wore sky-blue uniforms: some with puttees and steel helmets. The officers had high riding boots and the smart peaked képi. As the 'general of our horse' Bertram looked very dashing in a gold braided high-collared blue tunic and bright red breeches, while Parolles wore a delightfully frogged tunic. The III.v opening in Florence concentrated on evoking all the excitement generated by the victorious army as the Widow and Violenta stood upstage as on a loggia overlooking a Florentine street where muffled shouts and a military band could be heard — in 1981 Trevor Nunn brought the band on to the stage. Diana and Mariana sat on either side of the main stage until persuaded to join the fun and then all the girls ran back and forth, finally dragging the newly-arrived Helena up to look. As the unseen army passed before them the shouts grew louder and the music swelled. All were leaning right out only to rush back down to the main stage when Parolles apparently saw them and the music stopped.

Shelving's cloth for the officers' billet, where the plot to trap Parolles was hatched, depicted a stylised battered room with a window of cracked panes and shattered blinds. There was a practicable door set left of centre and the upper stage was furnished with a plain wooden table where the Dumaine brothers later sat (with glasses of champagne), to discuss Bertram's behaviour. Reviews suggest that the scenes of Parolles's capture and torment were very funny but sadly there are few details. In January 1928, Jackson referred to 'a setting suggestive of No Man's Land. The conversation on the field seemed to the audience quite ordinary and appropriate such as might easily have taken place between officers on the Western Front'.[9] In front of black velvet curtains, the soldiers, whispering and giggling, crouched down at the far left and right of the stage as they lay in wait for Parolles. The curtains drew back to reveal an Italian night sky as Parolles entered and reclined on the upper stage to wait until it was safe to go home. When he was set upon, he ran frantically up and down until he was finally caught and blind-folded and then he sank to his knees. The black curtains were briefly drawn while the first Dumaine gave orders to a soldier. The curtains drew back to discover Bertram standing outside the window of the Widow's loggia, leaning on the sill to woo Diana who remained securely on the other side. Again the black tabs came across for Diana's 'My mother told me just how he would woo'. Then the scene returned to the billet where Bertram joined his friends to drink champagne and boast of his conquest.

Parolles was brought on by three subalterns but in this modern setting was spared the indignity of the stocks. Blindfolded he stumbled down to the main stage as Bertram sat on the steps to listen to his former friend's lies. Ayliff cut most of the military details more familiar to an Elizabethan audience, and the most scurrilous slanders on the Dumaines. Crompton Rhodes praised Dan F. Roe as the interpreter for a 'little gem of comedy'. A photograph shows Parolles sitting on the floor staring up at his captors.[10] Amongst the group of soldiers stands a stolid figure wearing a steel helmet and puttees, holding the bandage which has been taken from the victim's eyes. As the black curtains drew across for the last time, Parolles was left alone to remove his cavalry sword and belt as he swore to be 'simply the thing I am'. He reappeared on the terrace at Rousillon, dressed in a shabby stained suit and clutching a battered trilby hat. Lavache came on singing to himself and shaking out a mat which he set down in the doorway while Parolles was left alone with Lafeu. George S. Wray, an experienced Shavian actor, was a bearded Lafeu, elegant in grey morning suit and spats. Crompton Rhodes commented: 'He made Lord Lafeu what he should be — witty, distinguished, a man of the world, the ironical commentator'.

The final scene was played as an after-dinner conversation on the terrace. A new marriage was arranged while the steward carried around a tray of coffee cups. The King, played by Grosvenor North, was now in a black frock coat. He had in general, Crompton Rhodes felt, brought 'humanity and distinction' to the role. Margaret Chatwin was 'not one of the Charleston grandmothers but a gentlewoman of the elder generation'. Charles Leighton as Rinaldo gave the impression of a very solid butler in winged collar and bow tie, dark tailcoat and trousers. Crompton Rhodes wrote that Diana, played by Jane Welsh, 'was alive and obviously enjoying herself at the whole mix up'. For the final scene she was tall and statuesque in an elegant dress and jacket with a fashionable cloche hat, while her mother looked very much the impoverished widow in a dowdy coat and hat and sensible shoes.

There appears to have been nothing equivocal about the ending of the play. When Helena appeared in a pretty but simple frock (no obvious signs of pregnancy), Bertram moved towards her on 'Both, both; O, pardon!'. She placed the ring on his finger and they embraced. The King's offer of a dowry for Diana was omitted and he spoke only the first and last two lines of his speech 'All yet seems well'. The actors arranged themselves around him for the Epilogue which was heralded by a flourish of trumpets. Finally they all bowed to the audience. It is certain that Bertram spoke his last lines quite sincerely, for the *Gazette*'s comment suggests: 'The interpretation of his closing lines is questionable; Shakespeare may have meant Bertram to be surprised into love for Helena . . . but more probably he meant him merely to make the best of a bad job'. Crompton Rhodes stated 'The end was quite touching . . . More eyes than those of Lord Lafeu "smelt onions" at it and wept. Mr Martin Walker made Count Bertram a pleasant sort of young man, not blessed with an excess of brains but very real . . . one felt he could have done a good deal worse than marry Helena'. The critic of the *Gazette* commented that Martin Walker looked 'exactly right — arrogant, heavy, embarrassed' but the review concluded that Walker needed to take a 'firmer hold on the part'. The *Evening Despatch* agreed 'He never seemed to be thoroughly inside the part and therefore was never really convincing except perhaps in the short love sequence on the balcony'. The role of the romantic bounder in the scene with Diana is relatively easy to play. As the unworthy object of Helena's love, Bertram presents more problems to the actor.

Eileen Beldon clearly benefited from the opportunity to play Helena naturalistically, and her performance was certainly not all bouncy self-confidence. The *Despatch* critic wrote 'She made an incredible person wholly credible and by doing so gave substance to the story. The stress of her anguish was profoundly moving and her lighter moods of deep interest'. The *Gazette* found her 'as convincing as Shakespeare and Bertram allowed her to be. The spontaneity and almost disconcerting naturalness of her acting (She is not afraid to be ugly when in tears) make her especially suited for such a part'. The general consensus was that the play had actually gained from modern costumes. The *Gazette* declared that:

> Soldiers, cynics and women seem to have changed little in 300 years . . . What is most important, we have a play that is modern in its whole tone and outlook. It asks questions and leaves them unanswered; it is cynical, destructive, bitter; it is in fact a modern problem play and had it been written in 1927 instead of 1603, its ethics would evoke long correspondences in the Press.

Earlier in the year, Jackson had compared himself to Frankenstein 'who created a mechanical monster far more powerful than he dreamed'.[11] The modern-dress idea had been taken up with great enthusiasm: not just for Shakespeare but for almost any period play which would normally require elaborate and expensive costuming. Jackson worried about reported attempts to present the precisely defined social milieux of Goldsmith and Sheridan in modern dress and was anxious that audiences should not be robbed of the enjoyment of beautiful period clothes. He feared that too much trivial modern detail would prove a distraction which would only lead to more ridicule poured on what were serious artistic experiments. Over and over again he emphasised that he wished to stress the timelessness of Shakespeare's plays but as his director and designer grew bolder in their evocation of twentieth-century civilisation, the challenge to audience perceptions, not only about Shakespeare but about their own society, grew more disturbing. Their experiments moved back to London in 1928 with two plays both staged at the Court Theatre. *The Taming of the Shrew*, which opened on 30 April was a triumph. It was one of the most successful Shakespearian productions of the decade. Three months earlier, in a first-night speech on 6 February, Jackson acknowledged that the modern-dress *Macbeth* had been a failure.

Ayliff's production of the *Shrew* had its origins in 1927 in an invitation to direct the play in New York at the Garrick Theatre with an American cast which included Basil Sidney as Petruchio and Mary Ellis as Katharine.[12] The New York production's triumphant reception must have been made all the sweeter by the knowledge that its 175 performances broke the record set for the *Shrew* by the arch-showman Daly forty years earlier. The reasons for the success both in New York, and in London with a homegrown cast, are not hard to find. On both sides of the Atlantic, the production was fast-moving and uproariously funny. Played in London and Birmingham by an integrated company of well-established repertory actors, it represented a victory for the entire repertory movement. The production achieved the apparent impossibility of popular success while adhering to the basic principles which had guided the production of Shakespeare by the Birmingham Company for nearly two decades.

With director and designer working in complete harmony, the Rep *Shrew* was visually delightful, combining wit and colour with economy of presentation. The Induction took place in Wincot, Warwickshire with a back-cloth revealing the glowing bar-parlour window of a traditional English ale-house complete with a hanging sign of 'The Swan'. There was just the suggestion of a frosty landscape at twilight. To the sound of crashes and bangs, the hostess, indignant in black bombazine, hurled Sly on to the stage. Frank Pettingell, a Chaplinesque Sly, slumped against one of the bold cut-out trees which framed the inn. The Lord (Laurence Olivier) and his party wore dashing hunting pink and when the players arrived their trunks bore the label 'Birmingham Repertory Company'. As Ivor Brown put it: 'At this point the note of civilised tomfoolery was struck and was never allowed to drop' (*Saturday Review*, 5 May 1928). The comic deception practised on Sly became even funnier when his 'mistress', played by Charles Lamb, was tastefully attired as a modern flapper with an Eton-cropped wig, flimsy sleeveless frock and matching heeled shoes. 'She' was seen with her arm draped around Sly as he spent the play proper in the stage box, alternating between rapt attention and drunken dozing which was reproved by the actors. His unaccustomed stiff collar crawled up his neck as he clutched a tankard which was replenished from a champagne bottle readily to hand.

Wincot moved to Padua and a stylised Italian street-cloth: a steeply rising flight of steps framed by a cut-out archway and the silhouette of rooftops. The house setting designed for Baptista was as simply furnished as always, but the windows overlooking cypress trees were hung with richly decorated curtains and the glossy table and chairs (specially supplied by a furniture shop) were adorned with fine marquetry. Petruchio's house and furniture, in complete contrast, were solid and plain. The final wedding feast took place in what some critics unkindly compared to a flashy Italian restaurant. The set was again backed with the first street-cloth but this time there were individual tables covered with lace cloths, flowers and fruit, little gilt chairs, streamers and Chinese lanterns.

The women's costumes were gorgeous. Katharine wore an evening dress of flame-coloured georgette, a day dress of emerald green marocain (a strong fabric to be tamed in) and a wedding dress of silver striped satin, gold embroidery and gold net. Bianca's evening dress was bright lemon yellow with a multi-layered skirt of gold-edged tulle, while the Widow wore magenta taffeta. At Katharine's wedding, the silent and usually invisible Widow (Chris Castor) looked stunning in a 'trousered gown' with hand-printed multi-coloured patterns on white crêpe de chine. There was also an unShakespearian 'Auntie' — a large elderly lady in a flowered hat — and a troupe of bridesmaids in more multi-layered tulle.

The unexpectedly glamorous widow was accompanied as usual by the other, now readily identifiable, minor characters. It is well-known that Ralph Richardson played Tranio as a cockney chauffeur aping the aristocrat with a posh 'Oxford' accent and dressed in morning coat and spats. Lucentio (Nigel Clarke), tutored and wooed Bianca in the guise of an earnest young curate. Most famously Curtis, traditionally a male Elizabethan rustic, became a tipsy lady housekeeper played by Drusilla Wills in a respectable long frock and black apron. The tailor (Antony Eustrel) was an oily,

132

exquisite Valentino figure. Indeed several reviews commented on how well the details of Elizabethan dress harmonised with modern fashions.

In fact the text itself presented few problems. Shakespeare, developing his skills as a comic dramatist, wrote in verse as clear and vigorous as the director could have wished. Ayliff cut most of the classical allusions and some specifically Elizabethan references, especially in the trading of riches between Bianca's competing suitors in II.i. Very occasionally, he enlivened long passages by dividing lines between several characters. For instance the Lord's long speech in the Induction, i 42–66, was spoken by several actors. Some of the Hortensio/Lucentio sub-plot was transposed for greater clarity. But in this production much of the comedy derived from the very incongruity of Shakespeare's text closely matched to modern characters and life styles. The music offered to Sly in the Induction came from a radio while the erotic pictures were displayed in a photograph album. Grumio's comment 'And that his bags shall prove' referred to trousers rather than money-bags and Curtis produced an electric heater when asked for a fire. Petruchio shouted an exasperated 'Come on, a God's name' to the starting handle of a battered Ford car. Most usefully, the description of Petruchio's bizarre wedding outfit became hilariously clear when he arrived in old riding breeches, a battered Fair Isle jersey, torn morning coat, one hunting boot, one Oxford shoe and a red handkerchief round his neck. Grumio was a comic-opera bandit, a mixture of black-shirted Fascist and Tom Mix, threatening the wedding guests with a gun. The more outrageous the comparison, the more the audience loved it.

Ayliff insisted that every piece of comic business came from the demands of the text translated into modern terms. A gum-chewing photographer recorded the events of Kate's wedding. Later a starved bride in Petruchio's house, she was tormented by a busily domestic Grumio who dusted a banana she was not allowed to eat. Petruchio added insult to injry when he lowered a single piece of macaroni into her mouth. St John Ervine was outraged and accused Ayliff of reducing Shakespeare's play to a vulgar farce (*Observer*, 6 May 1928). However physical rumbustiousness is inherent in the play. Katharine threatens to comb Hortensio's 'noddle with a three legged stool' and later (offstage) smashes a lute over his head. When Ayliff had her knock Hortensio's hat out of his hand or threaten Bianca with a hair brush and fell one of her bridesmaids with a well-aimed bouquet, the violent knock-about comedy could be seen as part of the fabric of the play. Some critics were shocked when Katharine was forced into an energetic wrestling match over Petruchio's knees. In a civilised modern world, a brutal story appeared to have even less credibility. The *Evening News* commented that 'short skirts and a shingle only emphasise the fact that Katharine today would probably be an aviator or a lion-tamer — anything, in fact, except a wife' (1 May 1928).

But when a blonde-ringletted Bianca, played by Muriel Hewitt as 'a melting fragment of goo-goo' (*Outlook*, 12 May 1928), was surrounded by her adoring suitors, Mary Pickford sprang to mind or more topically, Lorelei in Anita Loos's *Gentlemen Prefer Blondes*. As the entire wedding party chased the photographer down through the auditorium before the interval (the event appeared to be filmed by a newsreel camera man to add to the fun), the comic intimacy of a revue was conjured up. The car for Petruchio's journey back to Padua was a cut-out shape with wheels that revolved. When the back-cloth was moved horizontally the car appeared to move. The hapless Vincentio, making his entrance backwards on to the stage, was 'run over'. We are told that this music hall gag left the audience weak with laughter.[13] They were given access to Shakespeare, the popular dramatist, through the medium of the conventions of modern entertainment and consequently were able to enjoy the play on very much the same terms as the original audience.

At first sight it appears that Eileen Beldon and Scott Sunderland, as Katharine and Petruchio, did not attempt to find new depths in their characters, unlike Sybil Thorndike and Lewis Casson in the traditionally-dressed production at the Old Vic in 1927. Given Ayliff's directorial concentration on the overall texture of the production this is not surprising. But it is interesting to note that Sunderland brought an unusual restraint to his Petruchio. Ivor Brown commended an 'exquisitely light performance'. Throughout the play, even in the final scene when all the other actors wore evening dress, Petruchio appeared dressed in very plain-style tweed or flannel lounge suits in complete contrast to the self-conscious elegance displayed around him. The critic of the *Manchester Guardian* (1 May 1928) wrote 'Mr Sunderland gave an excellent impression of the modern adventurer who means to do a job of work as thoroughly as conscience insists and yet as airily as comedy demands'. The *Evening News* added 'there was always a smile behind his show of brutality'. William Dukes in the *Weekly Scotsman* (12 May 1928) made a startling observation on Sunderland's shrew-tamer: 'He lays emphasis on "all is done in reverend care of her". Nora Helmer would have been content with such a husband. He is more chivalrous than the moderns because he blames man and not woman for unhappy marriages'. Ayliff and Shelving's careful distinction in design and costume between the material values represented by Baptista's household and Petruchio pointed to the kind of moral values which years later Jonathan Miller attempted to explore in his productions in 1980 for BBC Television and in 1987 for the RSC.[14]

Eileen Beldon, playing the shrew with much vigorous sincerity, brought the same integrity to Katharine as to Helena. But after struggling with Petruchio she suddenly collapsed in tears, which caused Crompton Rhodes to remark that 'She had terrorised everybody by her termagancy but Petruchio had found her out' (*Birmingham Daily Post*, 1 May 1928). Her final speech was spoken beautifully, and, it seems, without a trace of irony. The play ended with 'God give you good night!'. Grumio, Tranio and Biondello entered carrying nightgowns and candles to light the way as the couples slowly exited. George Bishop recalls that Jackson had been tempted to end the play with the final lines of *The Taming of A Shrew* in which Sly wakes from his dream determined to tame his own wife.[15] The scene was rehearsed but the idea was eventually dropped. Instead the performance concluded on a more serious note of reconciliation and joy.

Ivor Brown, conscious of what he called 'the familiar solemnities' of past productions, admitted 'we do not laugh at what Shakespeare wrote but at the modern twist given to his writing. That, in my mind, is a great deal better than not laughing at all'. Hubert Griffiths, however, defended the production on other, rather surprising grounds. Always before, he claimed, he had dismissed the play as 'almost bestially lacking in sensitiveness . . . The modern production does not bear this out. It is still a farce — but a farce founded on a perfectly diabolical insight into character and still with its own application to the niceties of modern life' (*Evening Standard*, 1 May 1928). The age-old battle of the sexes now interlaced with a consciousness of feminist issues, made more acute by the granting, at long last in 1928, of the vote to all women over twenty-one. In the 'twenties this was treated to the cynical comic insights of dramatists like Somerset Maugham and Noël Coward: *Private Lives* with its cocktail mixture of sexual attraction and physical violence was first staged in 1930. Critics of Ayliff's *Shrew* were obliged to look at a Shakespearian heroine in the same visual context provided by modern accounts of gender relations. It is interesting that the simplistic response from some quarters — that modern women would not capitulate in the same way as Shakespeare's women — was everywhere contradicted by contemporary cultural and artistic mores.

However the cumulative effect of these first modern-dress ventures was the licence they gave other directors to experiment yet more freely with formerly hallowed texts. From 1927, at the Cambridge Festival Theatre, Terence Gray staged a series of wildly iconoclastic productions of Shakespeare. In 1929, at the Haymarket Theatre, Oscar Asche's modernisation of the text as well as the setting of *The Merry Wives of Windsor* seemed to some critics an outrageous but inevitable result. In the 'thirties, Theodore Komisarjevsky and Tyrone Guthrie shocked and delighted audiences with more modern-style productions. It could even be said that Ayliff and Jackson sowed the seed for musical comedy Shakespeare, especially Cole Porter's 1948 *Kiss Me Kate* based on *The Taming of the Shrew*.

In his account of the modern-dress *Shrew*, Norman Marshall justified the experiment because the play is 'so tedious and crude that it does not much matter what liberties the producer takes with it'. The modern-dress *Macbeth* failed, Marshall suggested, firstly because Shakespeare carefully set *Macbeth* in 'a primitive barbarous period' and secondly, because it was impossible to speak the passionate verse of the play naturalistically.[16] J. L. Styan supports this view: 'too much of this play is written in high style and too many of the speeches are rhetorical'.[17] Certainly, Ayliff's production of

Macbeth exposed the problems inherent in the modern-dress concept itself and the limitations of the directorial approach. But it must be stressed that the production was far from a complete failure. The critic of the *New Statesman* (11 February 1928), wrote a few days after the publication of the initial, largely derogatory, reviews:

> The present production of *Macbeth* is on the whole, the best production of *Macbeth* I have ever known . . . it might have been so superlatively good that we should have remembered it all our lives. The daily Press has not done justice to this production. It should have been stated that for the first time for generations an audience has been able to see Shakespeare's play scrubbed clean of the dust and varnish of ages and has discovered that what seemed remote and without significance is a living drama of extraordinary beauty and power. And how notable was the silence and attention of the audience.

The problem as he saw it was that 'a magnificent idea . . . if not spoilt, is at least dimmed and diminished in its execution'.

It is quite clear that the main reason for the failure was the casting of Eric Maturin as Macbeth. It appears that Jackson's 'no star' policy blew up in his face. Colin Keith-Johnston was an unconventional choice for Hamlet but, within the context of the production, it proved appropriate and he was an established member of the company. George Bishop tells us that Ayliff and Jackson had great difficulty in finding a suitable actor.[18] However, it is also possible that Ayliff did not want an experienced Shakespearian and that the choice of Maturin was part of a deliberate strategy. His only experience in Shakespeare had been the role of Osric in a New York production of *Hamlet* with Johnston Forbes-Robertson in 1904. In an article published in the *Weekly Despatch* on 5 February 1928 Jackson stated: 'If only actors would act naturally, Shakespeare would enjoy the greatest revival in history . . . They feel that "big" plays do not call for modern acting methods, that they must be done in stilted style. The best way I can help them is to produce the plays in modern dress and *make* them act naturally'. Given Ayliff's insistence that Shakespeare could be treated as a modern author and his interest in the human motivation at the heart of the play, it seems reasonable to assume that Ayliff was more concerned to present Macbeth as a man capable of a murderous act, rather than Macbeth the poet who just happens to be a murderer. One review described Maturin's particular talent: 'In parts that suit him, Mr Maturin is a brilliant actor. As a second rate blackmailer he is magnificent. I know no one who can better assume the supercilious tone of the West End saloon bar lounger — the kind who wants to take you to a night club he knows off Tottenham Court Road after closing time' (*Sunday Graphic*, 12 February 1928).

However, Macbeth's crime and subsequent damnation are expressed through verse and on this occasion the challenge to traditional assumptions was too daring. Maturin delivered the verse in a series of explosive gasps. Most notoriously 'blasted' in 'blasted heath' became an expletive. He turned 'thanks' into 'thengks'. The critic of the *Graphic* complained:

> Every other line is massacred by Mr Maturin's trick of intensifying his voice into a raucous whisper . . . This vocal failure is accompanied by an emotional failure no less marked. Mr Maturin did not exhibit the effect of his experience on his soul. He was the nearest thing to a Scottish gentleman in considerable difficulties that I ever hope to see.

Marshall's opinion that the play told the story of a barbaric act committed in a far-off primitive society was shared by most critics. Universal evil could have no place in a modern world. Ayliff himself seems to have been wary of some of the heightened poetic expression of the consequences of Macbeth's crime. The text was reasonably full with the loss of about two hundred lines including the Hecate scenes. But both accounts by Lennox and Ross in II.iii and II.iv of the unnatural events surrounding the death of Duncan were reduced to the most sketchy details. Macbeth's threat of universal chaos expressed to the witches in IV.i was reduced to five lines and Ross's description of the state of Scotland under Macbeth's rule in IV.iii, became merely 'Alas, poor country,/Almost afraid to know itself!'.

In a programme note, Jackson stressed that 'the people of Shakespeare are no different from ourselves'. He wanted to 'give to the tale of old unhappy far off things, the vividness and actuality of present day happenings'. But the adverse reaction had a good deal to do with the contemporary perception of twentieth-century progress. If Ophelia, Helena or Katharine, portrayed in the clothes of modern emancipated women, could not possibly be subject to their fathers or husbands, so a Scottish thane, dressed as a khaki-clad general, could not murder his king. Maturin wore military uniform throughout the performance, as did most of the other male characters.

The uniforms were painstakingly accurate down to the correct shape of the 'doublet' worn by Highland officers. Early in the play, Malcolm and Donalbain wore service tartan trews and caps. In Scotland, Macduff also wore trews but with a tam-o'-shanter and regimental plume. Both the bleeding sergeant and Seyton appeared as burly N.C.O.s with a khaki apron over their kilts and khaki webbing equipment for active service. Macbeth and Banquo sported the red tabs and gold braid on their caps to indicate their rank. Duncan, of course, was the Commander in Chief. Proponents of modern dress still consider that appropriate clothing is the best way of revealing social distinctions amongst Shakespeare's characters. It proved very useful in clarifying the servant/master relationship in the *Shrew*. But for *Macbeth* it was objected that modern military service dress concealed personality and reduced the wearers to a common level. There was also a disconcerting familiarity which made it difficult to accept brass-hatted staff officers speaking in verse. The *Sheffield Telegraph* summed up the prevailing feeling: 'It is not consistent with civilised notions that the general wishing to remove the King should stab him while he is a guest in the General's own house . . . G.O.C.s don't do such things' (15 February 1928). Newspaper critics seized every opportunity to exploit their sense of the ridiculous. There was a suggestion that Macbeth should have telephoned the news of Duncan's forthcoming arrival at Inverness. When the characters, clad in dressing gowns and pyjamas, assembled after Duncan's murder, the scene was reminiscent of a modern thriller. *Theatre World* (March 1928) insisted that in 1928, the murderer of Duncan would have been discovered and arrested within a few hours by the village constable. St John Ervine in the *Observer* was scathing: 'When I saw Malcolm lolling in front of the King of England's palace, I wondered why it was there were no newspapers, no telegraphs, no S.O.S. messages from the BBC to keep him informed of events in Scotland' (12 February 1928).

Shelving's designs were as brilliantly evocative of period and place as ever, perhaps too much so. In the *Shrew* the settings served to

139

enhance the creation of a comic world and delight the audience. In *Macbeth*, despite the simplicity of the means, the usual suggestiveness moved into a more concrete and disturbing statement. For *Hamlet* great care had been taken to present the play in as neutral a setting as possible. Now instead of plain front-cloths, Shelving produced stylised, but nevertheless very specific, representations of the envisaged locations. Duncan encountered the bleeding sergeant in front of a cloth which the prompt-book designates G.C.H.Q and which was obviously meant to depict the large wrought-iron gates, stone pillars and iron railings outside his palace. Lady Macbeth greeted Duncan before a cloth painted with the outline of her castle walls and a vista of hills beyond. The English scene was played very simply with just a stone bench set on the stage, but the backing cloth revealed a graceful tree overlooking the turrets and ramparts of what looked like Windsor Castle — a view which the prompt-book confirms. The precise association with Windsor created a particular tension between text and setting. Ayliff cut the English doctor's description of the English King's miraculous powers and the extended list of 'the King becoming graces'. But the problem remained that in 1928 there was no Scottish King and a singularly prosaic George V ruled over a United Kingdom. St John Ervine wondered whether Donalbain had fled to Ulster or the Irish Free State.

A few reviews of *Hamlet* had challenged Shelving to use completely modern furniture. For the interior of Macbeth's castle, the upper stage had a stone-like triple arched frame spanning three steps which led to the imposing door of the murder chamber. The main stage looked like a suburban drawing room. A cushioned divan with a purple brocade cover was placed downstage right. To the left stood a small elegant table which displayed some of the accoutrements of modern civilisation: a green shaded electric lamp, a whisky decanter and glass tumblers, a cigarette box and lighter and a potted plant.

The cloth for the state scenes at Dunsinane was dominated by two large windows, each hung with velvet curtains and with at least one practicable French door. There were small shaded lamps on either side of the false proscenium. When the second half of the play opened (at III.i), Banquo was seen up at the window apparently

140

watching the coronation procession which was accompanied by military band. Two thrones were placed below the steps. The dress uniforms and evening gowns worn by the new King and his court were in sharp contrast to the plain service khaki still worn by Banquo. Macbeth carried an enormous busby to complement his full ceremonial highland dress. Like his wife he wore an ermine-trimmed velvet cloak which he draped beside him on the throne while he interviewed the murderers. For the banqueting scene, there were three individual lace-covered tables and gilt chairs for the guests. An elaborate decorative mound of fruit, topped with a pineapple, stood on the centre table.

Edith Shackleton scorned the moment when Macbeth was able to interview a murderer unnoticed in such a setting and 'asked a silk upholstered dining chair to shake not its gory locks at him' (*Queen*, 15 February 1928). But others found the scene effective. Richard Jennings in the *Spectator* (11 February 1928), approved of the social embarrassment of the officially dressed guests. E. A. Baughan noticed the butler's 'quiet concern at the goings on of his master at the banquet' (*Daily News and Westminster Gazette*, 7 February 1928). Earlier Frank Pettingell as the portly bewhiskered butler, appeared gloriously drunk to play the Porter interlude in a ripe Scots accent. It was a moment which transcended time and costume and won unqualified approval. The treatment of the murderers was yet another valuable product of the emphasis on minor characters. James Agate, otherwise hostile to the production, praised the passionate conviction of 'the tiny but perfect performance' of Douglas Payne as the First Murderer (*Sunday Times*, 12 February 1928). He was a seedy down-at-heel valet while his companion (Ernest Stidwell) was a burly disgruntled sergeant. Seyton (Frank Moore) was the Third Murderer. Although 'Brass Hats' made unconvincing poets, characters like the bleeding Sergeant, Seyton and the Second Murderer gained a solidity and integrity from their N.C.O.'s uniforms.

Ayliff again enhanced the atmosphere of human familiarity with touches of naturalistic stage business. Gordon Crosse noticed that after the discovery of Duncan's body, Macbeth signalled his nervousness by lighting himself a cigarette and failing to offer a light to his guest, Lennox.[19] The doctor was summoned to administer a sedative to calm Macbeth's hysteria in the banqueting scene. The Queen waved him away and then took the glass to her husband before walking slowly upstage to open a window. The critic of the *Graphic* described Mary Merrall's performance at this moment: 'What could be more expressive and more evocative of human compassion than the restlessness of her eyes, never overdone, the deepening resignation with which she applies herself again to the task of looking after Macbeth again, the world of weariness she puts into the line "Almost at odds with morning, which is which"' (18 February 1928).

Before the opening night the catch-phrase 'Hamlet in plus-fours' had changed to 'Lady Macbeth in pyjamas'. Mary Merrall had to fight hard to control the audible titter provoked by her first appearance, in a short scarlet frock. Slight, fair, pale-faced and daintily dressed, she bore no resemblance to the traditional Lady Macbeth but unlike Maturin, she could command the verse and for many her performance was proof of what the production could have achieved. She had appeared with the Birmingham company in its early years, playing in *The Faithful* and *The Merchant of Venice*. Crompton Rhodes wrote: 'There was nothing hurried or tempestuous about the rendering, it moved forward with a steady purpose. No Lady Macbeth I have seen has ever shown better her dominance over Macbeth, physical and mental' (*Birmingham Daily Post*, 8 February 1928). Hubert Griffiths described her first scene when she read Macbeth's letter, half sitting, half lying on the divan: 'she took it more slowly than I would have believed possible . . . she revealed it to the listening audience as though it was a completely new piece of drama' (*Evening Standard*, 7 February 1928). She virtually seduced Macbeth into the murder of Duncan while an unseen gramophone played music from *Carmen* to entertain her royal guest. She sobbed on 'Art thou afeared/To be the same in thine own act and valour/As thou art in desire?'. She resisted Macbeth's attempts to embrace her when she said 'I have given suck' and finally reclined in his arms as she persuaded him to agree to her plan. It was she, however, who was the first to take a sedative before the murder (an aspirin, some unkind critics suggested). But by the sleep-walking scene, she seems to have won over her audience. She wore a simple lace-trimmed nightdress and carried a candlestick, so that her appearance proved to be no obstacle to her credibility.

In an opinion expressed in the *Daily Sketch* (8 March 1928), Bridges-Adams stated that modern men's suits made it impossible for a man to 'raise his hands above his head without looking a guy'. Hamlet or Macbeth, he maintained, could not be played without these extravagant physical gestures. 'This may seem a trivial comment, but after all the chief failing of the modern-dress school is the intrusion of trivialities'. A Shakespearian man or woman it seemed, was quite different in the physical expression of emotion from the buttoned-up gentry of twentieth-century Britain. Other observers, however, insisted that it was entirely feasible to convey the tragic plight of a Shakespearian character in decorous modern settings and clothes. Many agreed with J. K. Prothero in *G.K.'s Weekly* (25 February 1928): 'The agreeable home-like atmosphere, the cheeky little boy, the petulant woman . . . the spectacle of a mother in a simple country bungalow talking to her child, suddenly and ruthlessly sent to death, has a fresh significance'. The same writer admired Laurence Olivier's Malcolm, played as a young and eager boy. For the scene in England, uniforms were abandoned in favour of tweed plus-fours for Ross and lounge suits for Malcolm and Macduff. Scott Sunderland as Macduff, in a performance which was one of the highlights of the production, for once had a hat, a trilby which he pulled down over his brows to hide his grief. The scene was universally praised. Protheroe wrote that it was 'admirably rendered. Costume calls for florid gestures. Modern dress induces a restraint the more effective when emotion breaks it through'. A review in *New Age* (16 February 1928) refused to treat the production as an exercise in triviality. The writer focused on the attempt 'to render didactic verse intimate and conversational'. The introduction of a Scots accent for some characters, he suggested, actually assisted in articulation and understanding. He singled out both Eileen Beldon (Lady Macbeth's gentlewoman), and Laurence Olivier for their effective verse speaking. From Olivier 'the speeches were conversational and sincere — and still poetry'.

The *New Age* critique found the speeded-up final scenes, staged as a modern battle, less ludicrous than usual. But other reviews simply scoffed. When Macbeth received the news of Malcolm's advance he was seated at a bulky carved table downstage of a back-cloth showing a large window overlooking mist-shrouded hills. Malcolm's scenes with his army were played before a front curtain which enabled the Dunsinane set to be changed for the last time to show a twisted shattered window and furniture piled up to form a makeshift barricade from which the soldiers fired. Gordon Crosse noted that Macbeth's 'charmed life' seemed all the more convincing when soldiers blazed away at him with revolvers.[19] Macbeth only resorted to his cavalry sword to fight with Macduff when his gun failed him. The British Acoustics Film Company went to Aldershot to record the authentic sound of artillery batteries and machine guns.

It seems curious now that the generation which had endured the carnage of the First World War should have been unconscious of the implications of Shakespeare's text married to the sights and sounds of modern battle. *Journey's End*, the only successful play to come from the experience of war-time suffering, was still ten months away from its first performance.[20] Jackson was later to regret rejecting it for his company. In *Macbeth*, the realistic clamour of ebbing war had opened the play. Shelving's vivid expressionistic back-cloth depicted the shattered sails of a ruined windmill which were gauntly silhouetted against the sky. Some critics were impressed while others dismissed it as 'Flanders à la mode'. A later historian of the Rep, T. C. Kemp, wrote in 1943: 'It is possible that had *Macbeth* been put on in modern dress, in say, 1941, when Nazi butchery was at its height, when "vaulting ambition" was wading through slaughter toward world domination, then the spectacle of massacre in modern dress would not have appeared so distorted'.[21]

Viewed from the perspective of more than half a century, the appearance of the witches seems extraordinarily powerful. Muriel Aked, Joan Pereira and Una O'Connor played them as old, derelict women with straggling grey hair and bristly chins. Costumes included an old jacket tied with string and fastened with a safety pin, a battered tweed hat, rusty bonnets and ragged shawls. For the apparition scene Shelving used a gauze to obscure the shape of the witches's hovel. The faintly glimmering apparitions appeared to rise out of a leaping fire. But for many in the Court audience the witches were too real: as familiar as their own charladies. Even the ingredients for the spell were rather too palpable: the sow's blood, for example, was administered from a whisky bottle. St John Ervine

144

derided the weird sisters as 'three gin-sodden hags from the Canongate'. Yet in 1933 for his Stratford production of *Macbeth*, Theodore Komisarjevsky translated the witches into horrible old women plundering an eerily modern battlefield.

Granville Barker dismissed the modern-dress concept as merely 'a purge and a tonic to the sluggish-fancied spectator',[22] however T. C. Kemp, with the benefit of hindsight, stated in 1943 that the first experiment with *Cymbeline* assisted at 'the initiation of psychological as well as sartorial reform in the presentation of Shakespeare'.[23] If the productions did nothing else they offered a liberating alternative to tradition for directors and audiences alike. Clearly there were lessons to be learned. Audiences were happiest when they were allowed to forget the costuming, and Shelving was perhaps drifting too near the old conventions of representational décor. Mary Merrall had demonstrated that skilful verse speaking need not clash with a modern approach to character.

By treating Shakespeare as a modern dramatist, Ayliff had revealed the continuities of both human and theatrical experience. But for the insight derived from the modern-dress experiments to be realised more fully, there had to be further cultural and psychological change in both playgoers and playmakers. The drama written after the Second World War reflected a society chastened by the experience of evil and less confident of the inevitability of human progress. The rigid dividing lines between genres began to blur. A nondescript salesman could be a tragic figure and a destitute beggar a symbol of instability and potential power. In the 'thirties and 'forties there were fresh attempts to revive verse drama in the plays of T. S. Eliot, W. H. Auden and Christopher Fry, but ultimately the new dramatic poetic voice came in prose rather than verse. The prose of dramatists like Beckett and Pinter created a language which was as flexible, allusive and linguistically rich as Shakespeare's own. Scholarly work on Shakespeare's dramatic techniques and his use of image and symbol contributed a deeper understanding of his achievement. The notion that Shakespeare could be 'our contemporary' took on even greater validity. The successors of Ayliff and Jackson could build more surely on the foundations laid by the first modern-dress experiments.

Ayliff's *Macbeth* and *The Taming of the Shrew* were brought to

145

Birmingham towards the end of 1928 but with different casts. *Macbeth*, which opened on 3 November, had Jack Twyman in the title role and by all accounts he gave a more competent performance than Eric Maturin. The *Shrew* was a joyful New Year romp which opened on 31 December with Harry Wilcoxon as Petruchio and Daphne Heard as Katharine. *Othello*, the final production in this sequence of modern-dress experiments, had its first night on Saturday, 23 February 1929. Scott Sunderland played Othello to Daphne Heard's Desdemona. Julian D'Albie and Eileen Beldon played Iago and Emilia. No prompt-book has survived; there are no photographs and few reviews. There was little time for rehearsal (Ayliff was ill during the final stages) and the production ran, as usual, for just two weeks. The critic of *The Stage* judged Shelving's settings to be 'simple, effective and full of bright colour' (25 February 1929). Crompton Rhodes decided that when performed in modern dress, Othello's psychological breakdown took on a greater credibility but that the updating did little to hide the play's melodramatic qualities. His review ended on a wistful note: 'The modern-dress method imposes a solidity of setting which is not quite so satisfactory as Sir Barry's old Elizabethan compromises' (*Birmingham Daily Post*, 25 February 1929).

But Shakespeare experiment stopped abruptly. Between 1929 and 1943 when Ayliff revived his modern-dress *Shrew* (Margaret Leighton played Kate to an elderly Scott Sunderland's Petruchio) there were only two productions of Shakespeare at the Rep, both directed by Herbert Prentice: a modern-dress *Hamlet* with Stephen Murray as the Prince in 1935 and a lavishly-dressed and set *A Midsummer Night's Dream* presented for Christmas 1936. During the early 'thirties Jackson's managerial affairs were extraordinarily complex as companies played in London and Birmingham and undertook both British and overseas tours. He also presented the annual Malvern Festival, inaugurated in August 1929 with the première of Shaw's *The Apple Cart*. What began in Malvern as a fortnight's festival devoted to Shaw became in later years a highly prestigious literary event. Artists and scholars gathered for a month in Malvern to discuss, lecture, listen to music and attend plays produced as an historical cycle of English drama. While there was no Shakespeare there were such rarities as *The Play of the Wether*, *Ralph*

Roister Doister, A Woman Killed with Kindness and *Gammer Gurton's Needle*, all directed and designed by Ayliff and Shelving. The absence of Shakespeare at the Rep itself was mirrored throughout provincial theatres where the struggle to survive in the midst of the Depression replaced the impulse to achieve radical theatrical change. Indeed only Komisarjevsky's five iconoclastic productions at the Shakespeare Memorial Theatre between 1932 and 1939 reminded provincial audiences of the possibilities of innovation. Exciting ensemble-based Shakespeare was to be found, however, in London, at the Old Vic under Harcourt Williams and Tyrone Guthrie; in productions directed by John Gielgud and Michel Saint-Denis in West End theatres; in the Open Air Theatre in Regent's Park and in Robert Atkins' experiments with Elizabethan staging at The Ring in Blackfriars. The success of these metropolitan ventures, often undertaken by former Rep protégés, served to further the principles long established in Birmingham. Respect for the integrity of Shakespearian texts, fast-moving, evenly-balanced performance, simple evocative design which enhanced rather than overwhelmed plays, and the consciousness that Shakespearian themes could illuminate modern preoccupations, had become the norm rather than the exception. While Jackson and his colleagues appeared to have exhausted their capacity to create new options in Shakespeare production, the example of their work continued to act as leaven for the future.

147

Epilogue

My first experience of Shakespeare in performance was Douglas Seale's production of *Henry V*, staged at the Rep in February 1957. I can remember nothing except the excitement it generated, but as a result I was hooked on Shakespeare for life. I now know that this *Henry V*, with Albert Finney in the title role, was the last in a remarkable series of Shakespeare productions directed by Seale which began in 1948 with a rumbustious, masked *The Comedy of Errors* and included *Pericles* in 1954 and *Richard II* in 1955. Between 1951 and 1953, working with Jackson who prepared the texts, he staged the three plays of *Henry VI*. What began as a tentative venture with *Part Two* in 1951, gathered momentum until the complete Trilogy was mounted in Birmingham and London in 1953. After witnessing the performances at the Old Vic Kenneth Tynan wrote: 'The plays live in my mind as a series of savage tableaux, each held and lit for a moment as by a magnesium flare . . . Pound for pound, this is the most vigorous Shakespearean company in England' (*Evening Standard*, 17 July 1953).

For Sir Barry Jackson, such an accolade must have seemed ample justification for his policies in the early fifties. These were the years when the theatre in general was dominated by glossy West End values and star actors. In an article 'On Producing *Henry VI*' published in 1953, Jackson outlined his case for the kind of Shakespeare production which his theatre had promoted since 1913:

The condition of the theatre, an intimate-sized auditorium with a company of young artists, who make up in zest and loyalty for what they may lack in their more publicised comrades is to me the ideal line

148

of attack required for the poet's plays. They all demand youthful vigour and drive. Some of the subtleties, the results of age and experience, may be missing, but I willingly sacrifice these for forthright exposition. There comes a time when subtleties of production and star mannerisms grow to such a proportion that the main theme vanishes into oblivion.[1]

In 1948, his refusal to submit to money-making pressures had led to his resignation as Director of the Shakespeare Memorial Theatre. The 'stars-policy' subsequently operated by his successors Anthony Quayle and Glen Byam Shaw brought highly lucrative prestige to a theatre which hitherto had been treated with studied indifference by the metropolitan establishment. But with hindsight it is now possible to see that Jackson's work in Stratford laid the foundations for the Royal Shakespeare Company's present international reputation. Recently Sir Peter Hall has said of the Royal Shakespeare Theatre: 'Barry Jackson in a sense started it all because he turned this place at the end of the War from being a rather overgrown 1930s building that housed a number of actors for short seasons into a production company that could make sets and costumes' (*Observer*, 28 June 1992). In so doing Jackson was preparing for the kind of company which Archer, Shaw and Granville Barker dreamed about at the beginning of the century: a company where secure contracted artists could have the luxury of long rehearsal periods and the chance to develop and mature performances played in true repertoire. What perhaps no-one could have foreseen was that this success would begin to threaten the kind of regional repertory Shakespeare production which trained young actors before the era of nationally-subsidised, monolithic institutions like the RSC and the Royal National Theatre. Certainly by 1961 when Barry Jackson died, my own attention was turning away from the Rep towards the Royal Shakespeare Company which Hall inaugurated in 1960. I only saw two more productions of Shakespeare at Birmingham Rep in the 'sixties — John Harrison's 1962 *The Tempest* (Derek Jacobi played Ferdinand), and Braham Murray's 1965 *The Winter's Tale*.

As I have stressed, innovation in Shakespeare production at the beginning of the Rep's history owed much to a parallel emphasis on modern drama and stagecraft. This of course was Peter Hall's policy when he founded the RSC. During the late 'fifties it was obvious that Jackson was increasingly out of sympathy with modern theatre. In 1956 he described a recent visit to the Royal Court Theatre, now the home of the English Stage Company, and once the venue for Jackson's own radicalism over thirty years before:

> It was very noisy. Young people shouting and behaving in a most extraordinary fashion. It left me completely cold. Before the play I looked around at the audience. Girls with pale emaciated faces and long black hair. Young men in dirty slacks and pullovers and beards, with pipes. No, I think there is something more solid in the theatre than the type of play I saw there . . . Fantasy, we could do with more of that. Finesse, wit and profundity, particularly profundity. (*Wolverhampton Express and Star*, 24 May 1956)

The power of Jackson's influence, even after death, combined with the limited technical resources of a now out-dated theatre and competition from Stratford, created problems for the management in the early 'sixties. John Harrison, however, who was Artistic Director from 1962 until 1966, completed the canon of Rep Shakespeare with productions of *Troilus and Cressida, Henry VIII* and *Titus Andronicus* in 1963 — Derek Jacobi played Troilus, Henry VIII and Aaron. When Peter Dews became Artistic Director in 1966 he ruthlessly set about modernising the theatre's policy. There was a real sense of the wheel coming full circle — back to the energy and optimism of the earliest years. Once more what was best of the old was yoked with the new. Also the Rep had a director who, for all his professionalism, had the true amateur's love of acting. Not since the first decade of the Rep's existence had the director been seen so frequently on the stage. In 1967 when Dews came to direct his first Rep Shakespeare he made a significant, almost symbolic decision to remove the front row of auditorium seats and rebuild the apron stage discarded in the 'thirties. A programme note for *Richard II* states: 'The need now is to narrow the gap between actor and audience, to come out to meet the challenge, lessen the work and increase the impact'. His greatest success that year was in the time-honoured tradition of modern-dress Shakespeare: a witty, Carnaby Street *As You Like It* with vibrant designs by Pamela Howard and Brian Cox as Orlando. In 1968 Cox played Iago to Michael

Gambon's Othello. In 1969 Dews made the typically outrageous decision to invite the American television idol Richard Chamberlain to play Hamlet — the first American actor to play the part in England since John Barrymore. Audiences flocked to the Rep and J. C. Trewin wrote that 'Sir Barry would have been uncommonly pleased — flattered indeed for Chamberlain's decision confirms the international renown of the Repertory' (*Birmingham Post*, 5 December 1968). It is debatable whether Jackson would have been pleased at the commercial showman's instincts behind the project, but Chamberlain himself was honoured by the invitation. More important was the fact that Dews was continuing the tradition of training young actors in Shakespeare performance. Michael Gambon, who had worked in the newly-formed National Theatre Company under Sir Laurence Olivier, was sent by Olivier to complete his apprenticeship at the Rep. As Gambon later recalled: 'A year after I'd walked on as a messenger in his *Othello*, I was playing the name part and he sent me a good luck telegram. My fellow actors didn't believe it was genuine'.[2]

In 1971 the company moved into a new building conceived at a time of optimism, when a larger theatre seemed a priority, and born into a bleak age of economic recession. State and civic subsidy, which was only a dream at the beginning of the century, has only partially helped the new Rep to combat recurring crises in regional arts provision. In 1987 the drama critic Michael Billington claimed that the impoverishment of the arts was responsible for the relative neglect of Shakespeare production in the regions.[3] Now in the 'nineties there's a new phenomenon: touring productions of Shakespeare often in radical adaptations. In 1991 I saw an adaptation of *Measure for Measure* called *Dear Isabel* presented at the Old Rep by members of the Birmingham-based Custard Factory Company. As the three actors performed against a simple curtained background on Barry Jackson's stage, it seemed that they were continuing a tradition for experiment which that theatre had represented for sixty years. It was a hopeful sign.

Appendix
Chronological List of Productions

1: Birmingham

Play	Director	Designer	First performance
1913			
Twelfth Night	Barry Jackson	Barry Jackson	15 February
King John	Arnold Pinchard	Barry Jackson	19 April
The Merry Wives of Windsor	John Drinkwater	Barry Jackson	23 April
The Merchant of Venice	John Drinkwater	Barry Jackson	7 June
Henry IV, Part I	Arnold Pinchard	Barry Jackson	11 October
1914			
As You Like It	Harcourt Williams	Barry Jackson	7 February
Twelfth Night	Barry Jackson	Barry Jackson	20 April
1915			
The Tempest	John Drinkwater	Barry Jackson	17 April
The Merchant of Venice	John Drinkwater	Barry Jackson	16 October
1916			
The Tempest	John Drinkwater	Barry Jackson	22 April

The Merry Wives of Windsor	John Drinkwater	Barry Jackson	24 April
Macbeth	John Drinkwater	Barry Jackson	29 April
Twelfth Night	John Drinkwater	Barry Jackson	2 May
The Merchant of Venice	John Drinkwater	Barry Jackson	3 May
As You Like It	Harcourt Williams	Barry Jackson	15 May

1917

The Merry Wives of Windsor	John Drinkwater	Barry Jackson	7 April
Twelfth Night	John Drinkwater	Barry Jackson	23 April
The Two Gentlemen of Verona	John Drinkwater	Barry Jackson	28 April

1918

Measure for Measure	John Drinkwater	Barry Jackson	23 April
The Merry Wives of Windsor	John Drinkwater	Barry Jackson	2 May
Twelfth Night	John Drinkwater	Barry Jackson	9 May
The Taming of the Shrew	John Drinkwater	Frank D. Clewlow	15 June

1919

Twelfth Night	Barry Jackson	Barry Jackson	19 April
Much Ado About Nothing	Conal O'Riordan & Eric Messiter	Guy Kortright & Barry Jackson	3 May
The Merchant of Venice	Barry Jackson	Barry Jackson	24 May
Love's Labour's Lost	Barry Jackson	Barry Jackson	22 November
As You Like It	Barry Jackson	Barry Jackson	1 December

1920

Love's Labour's Lost	Barry Jackson	Barry Jackson	23 April
Othello	A. E. Filmer	Paul Shelving	5 May
Much Ado	Conal O'Riordan	Guy Kortright	15 May

About Nothing	& Eric Messiter	& Barry Jackson	
Henry IV, Part I	Barry Jackson	Barry Jackson	27 November
The Merry Wives of Windsor	A. E. Filmer	Paul Shelving	27 December

1921

Henry IV Part I	Barry Jackson	Barry Jackson	18 April
Henry IV Part II	Barry Jackson	Barry Jackson	23 April

1922

Twelfth Night	H. K. Ayliff	Barry Jackson	23 April
*Romeo and Juliet***	H. K. Ayliff	Paul Shelving	27 May

1923

Cymbeline	H. K. Ayliff	Paul Shelving	21 April

1924

The Two Gentlemen of Verona	H. K. Ayliff	Paul Shelving	22 November

1925

Love's Labour's Lost	E. Stuart Vinden	Barry Jackson	11 April
*Hamlet**	H. K. Ayliff	Paul Shelving	9 November

1926

— — — —

1927

All's Well that Ends Well	H. K. Ayliff	Paul Shelving	16 April

1928

*Macbeth**	H. K. Ayliff & Matthew Forsyth	Paul Shelving	3 November

154

The Taming of the Shrew*	H. K. Ayliff & Matthew Forsyth	Paul Shelving	31 December

1929

Othello	H. K. Ayliff	Paul Shelving	23 February

2: London

1924 Regent Theatre

Romeo and Juliet	H. K. Ayliff	Paul Shelving	22 May

1925 Kingsway Theatre

Hamlet	H. K. Ayliff	Paul Shelving	25 August

1928 Royal Court Theatre

Macbeth	H. K. Ayliff	Paul Shelving	6 February
The Taming of the Shrew	H. K. Ayliff	Paul Shelving	30 April

Selected Bibliography

Published Material

Archer, William, *About the Theatre* (London, 1886).
    'A Plea for an Endowed Theatre', *Fortnightly Review* Vol. 45, New Series (1 January–1 June 1889), pp. 610–626.
    Study and Stage (London, 1899).
Archer, William and Harley Granville Barker, *A National Theatre: Schemes and Estimates* (London, 1907).
Arnold, Matthew, 'The French Play in London', *Irish Essays* (London, 1891), pp. 150–175.
Aslin, Elizabeth, *The Aesthetic Movement* (London, 1969).
Beauman, Sally, *The Royal Shakespeare Company: A History of Ten Decades* (Oxford, 1982).
Barker, Harley Granville, *The Exemplary Theatre* (London, 1922).
    'Introduction to *Cymbeline*', *The Player's Shakespeare* Vol. II (London, 1923), pp. ix–vii.
    'Introduction to *Macbeth*', *The Player's Shakespeare* Vol. III (London, 1923), pp. ix–ix.
    Prefaces to Shakespeare, First Series (London, 1927).
Berry, Ralph, 'The Aesthetics of Beerbohm Tree's Shakespeare Festivals', *Nineteenth Century Theatre Research* Vol. 9, No. 1 (Summer, 1981), pp. 23–51.
Bingham, Madeline, *The Great Lover: the Life and Art of Herbert Beerbohm Tree* (London, 1978).
Bishop, George, *My Betters* (London, 1957).
    Barry Jackson and the London Theatre (London 1933; reissued New York, 1969).
Bland, Alan, ed., *The Gong*, Birmingham Repertory Theatre Monthly Periodical (December 1921–December 1922).

Selected Bibliography

Braun, Edward, *The Director and the Stage* (London, 1982).

Bridie, James, *One Way of Living* (London, 1939).

Briggs, Asa, *History of Birmingham* Vol. II, *1865–1938* (London, 1952).

Byrne, M. St Clare, 'Fifty Years of Shakespearian Production: 1898–1948', *Shakespeare Survey* Vol. 2 (1949), pp. 1–20.

Carter, Huntly, *The New Spirit in Drama and Art* (London, 1912).

The Theatre of Max Reinhardt (London, 1914).

Casson, Lewis, 'William Poel and the Modern Theatre' *The Listener* (10 January 1952), pp. 56–68.

Cheney, Sheldon, *The New Movement in the Theatre* (New York, 1914).

Chisholm, Cecil, *Repertory, An Outline of the Modern Theatre Movement* (London, 1934).

Craig, Edward, *Gordon Craig*, (London, 1968).

'E. W. Godwin and the Theatre', *Theatre Notebook* Vol. 31, No. 2 (1977), pp. 30–33.

Craig, Edward Gordon, *The Mask* Vol. 1–15 ed. Edward Gordon Craig (Florence, 1908–29).

On the Art of the Theatre (London, 1911; reissued London, 1957).

Scene (London, 1923).

Dean, Basil, *Seven Ages* (London, 1970).

Devlin, Diana, *A Speaking Part: Lewis Casson and the Theatre of his Time* (London, 1982).

Donaldson, Frances, *The Actor Managers* (London, 1970).

Drinkwater, John, *The Gentle Art of Theatre Going* (London, 1927).

Inheritance (London, 1931).

Discovery (London, 1932).

Fitzgerald, Percy, *Shakespearean Representation: Its Laws and Limits*, (London, 1908).

Fraser, Claude Lovat, 'The Art of the Theatre', *The Studio*, Vol. 82 (November 1921), pp. 210–212.

Fry, Charlton, F., *Charles Fry, his Life and Work* (London, 1932).

Furnivall, F. J., 'Opening Address for New Shakspere Society (30 March 1874), *New Shakspere Society Transactions* (1874).

Gielgud, John, *Early Stages* (London, 1939).

An Actor and His Time (London, 1979).

Gill, Maud, *See the Players* (London, 1938).

Glasstone, Victor, *Victorian and Edwardian Theatre* (London, 1975).

Goldie, Grace Wyndham, *The Liverpool Repertory Theatre* (London, 1935).

Guthrie, Tyrone, *A Life in the Theatre* (London, 1961).

Hardwicke, Cedric, *Let's Pretend* (London, 1932).

A Victorian in Orbit (London, 1961)

Haring-Smith, Tori, *From Farce to Metadrama: A Stage History of 'The Taming of the Shrew' 1594–1983* (Westport, 1985).

Harker, Joseph, *Studio and Stage* (London, 1924).

Howe, P. P., *The Repertory Theatre: A Record and a Criticism* (London, 1910).

Hughes, Alan, *Henry Irving, Shakespearean* (Cambridge, 1981).

Hunter, Thos. F., 'Some Notes on the Staging of *Julius Caesar*', *The Stage Year Book* 1914 (London, 1914), pp. 45–56.

Innes, Christopher, *Edward Gordon Craig* (Cambridge, 1983).

Jackson, Anthony and George Rowell, *The Repertory Movement: A History of Regional Theatre in Britain* (Cambridge, 1984).

Jackson, Sir Barry, 'Costume', *The Robes of Thespis* ed. for Rupert Mason by George Sheringham and R. Boyd Morrison (London, 1928), pp. 65–70.

    Review of Robert Speaight's *William Poel and the Elizabethan Revival*, *Shakespeare Quarterly* Vol. 6 (1955), pp. 89–90.

    'Producing *Henry VI*', *Shakespeare Survey* Vol. 6 (1953), pp. 49–52.

    'Producing the Comedies', *Shakespeare Survey* Vol. 8 (1955), pp. 74–80.

Jackson, Russell, 'E. W. Godwin and Wilson Barrett's *Hamlet* of 1884', *Jahrbuch, Deutsches Shakespeare-Gesellschaft West* (1974), pp. 186–200.

    'Shakespeare in Liverpool: Edward Saker's Revivals 1876–81', *Theatre Notebook* Vol. 32, No. 3 (1978), pp. 100–109.

    'Perfect Types of Womanhood', *Shakespeare Survey* Vol. 32 (1979), pp. 15–26.

Kemp, T. C., *The Birmingham Repertory Theatre* (Birmingham, 1948).

Kemp, T. C., and J. C. Trewin, *The Stratford Festival* (Birmingham, 1953).

Kennedy, Dennis, *Granville Barker and the Dream of Theatre* (Cambridge, 1985).

Lee, Sir Sidney, *Shakespeare and the Modern Stage* (London, 1906).

Lewis, Peter, *The National: A Dream Made Concrete* (London, 1990).

Macgowan, Kenneth, *The Theatre of Tomorrow* (London, 1923).

Marshall, Norman, *The Other Theatre* (London, 1947).

    The Producer and the Play (London, 1957; reissued London, 1975).

Martin-Harvey, Sir John, *Autobiography* (London, 1932).

Matthews, Bache, *A History of the Birmingham Repertory Theatre* (London, 1924).

Mazer, Carey, *Shakespeare Refashioned: Elizabethan Plays on Edwardian Stages* (Ann Arbor, 1981).

Meisel, Martin, *Realizations: Narrative, Pictoral and Theatrical Arts in Nineteenth-century England* (Princeton, 1983).

Merchant, W. Moelwyn, *Shakespeare and the Artist* (London, 1959).

Montague, C. E. *Dramatic Values* (London, 1910).

Mullins, Donald C., *The Development of the Playhouse* (Berkeley, 1970).

O'Connor, Garry, *Ralph Richardson: An Actor's Life* (London, 1982).

Odell, George C. D., *Shakespeare from Betterton to Irving*, Vol. II (New York, 1920; reissued New York, 1966).

Palmer, John, '*Hamlet* in Modern Dress', *Fortnightly Review* No. 707, New Series (2 November 1925), pp. 674–683.

Payne, Ben Iden, *A Life in A Wooden O* (New Haven, 1977).

Poel, William, *Shakespeare in the Theatre* (London, 1913).

Monthly Letters (London, 1929).

Pogson, Rex, *Miss Horniman and the Gaiety Theatre, Manchester* (London, 1952).

Price, Joseph, *The Unfortunate Comedy: A Study of 'All's Well That Ends Well' and its Critics* (Liverpool, 1968).

Purdom, C. B., *Granville Barker* (London, 1955).

Rhodes, R. Crompton, *The Stagery of Shakespeare* (Birmingham, 1922).

Ridge, C. Harold, *Stage Lighting* (Cambridge, 1928).

Rosenfeld, Sybil, *A Short History of Stage Design in Great Britain* (Oxford, 1973).

'Some Experiments of Beerbohm Tree', *Nineteenth Century Theatre Research*, Vol. 1, No. 2 (Autumn 1974), pp. 75–83.

'Hubert Herkomer's Theatrical Theories and the New Stagecraft', in *The Triple Bond: Plays mainly Shakespearean in Peformance*, ed. Joseph Price (University Park, 1975), pp. 274–279.

Salberg, Derek, *Ring Down the Curtain* (Luton, 1980).

Salmon, Eric, *Granville Barker: A Secret Life* (London, 1983).

Salmon, Eric, ed. *Granville Barker and his Correspondents* (Detroit, 1986).

Schultz, Stephen C., 'Two Notes on William Poel's Sources', *Nineteenth Century Theatre Research*, Vol. 2, No. 2 (Autumn, 1874), pp. 85–90.

Senelick, Laurence, *Gordon Craig's Moscow 'Hamlet'* (Westport, 1982).

Shaw, George Bernard, *Our Theatres in the Nineties* Vol. II (London, 1932).

Shelving, Paul, 'Stage Design', *Theatre World* (January 1927), p. 22.

Shipp, Horace, 'The Artist in the Dressing Room', *The Robes of Thespis* ed. for Rupert Mason by George Sheringham and R. Boyd Morrison (London, 1928) pp. 137–143.

Speaight, Robert, *William Poel and the Elizabethan Revival* (London, 1954).

Stokes, John, *Resistible Theatres: Enterprise and Experiment in the late Nineteenth Century* (London, 1972).

Styan, J. L., *The Shakespeare Revolution: Criticism and Performance in the Twentieth Century* (Cambridge, 1977).

Trewin, J. C., *Benson and the Bensonians* (London, 1960).

The Birmingham Repertory Theatre 1913–1963 (London, 1963).

Shakespeare on the English Stage (London, 1964).

Peter Brook (London, 1971).

Walton, J. Michael, ed. *Craig on Theatre* (London, 1983).

Wells, Stanley, *Royal Shakespeare* (Manchester, 1977).

Williams, E. Harcourt, *Four Years at the Old Vic* (London, 1935).

Williams, Simon, *Shakespeare on the German Stage* Vol. I: *1586–1914* (Cambridge, 1990).

Unpublished Material

Held in the Birmingham Repertory Theatre Archive, Birmingham Central Library

Birmingham Repertory Theatre prompt-books, press-clippings books, programmes and photographs.

Sir Barry Jackson, unpublished speeches in typescript (in chronological order).

Speech to the Sheffield Playgoers' Society, 12 November 1913.

'The Theatre in the Grip of the Box Office', undated.

'Literature and the Drama', 1920.

'The Artist and the Theatre', speech to Birmingham Art Circle, 1921.

'What We Did', 1921.

'The Repertory Movement', 1932.

Letter from William Poel to Sir Barry Jackson, 26 August 1925.

Typescript of radio broadcast: 'The Mighty Line' by T. C. Kemp, broadcast 19 November 1947.

Held in Shakespeare Library, Birmingham Central Library

'Shakespearean performances which I have seen', from January 1890 to July 1953, by Gordon Crosse, manuscript diaries, 21 Vols. (1890–1953).

Birmingham Shakespeare Reading Club.

A collection of newspaper cuttings, leaflets, tickets etc., relating to the Birmingham Shakespeare Reading Club 1871–1903.

Birmingham University Shakespeare Society.

General material 1906–1908.

Selected Bibliography

Further unpublished material

Letter from Sir Barry Jackson to William Poel, 28 August 1925 (MS 32A, Kenneth Spencer Research Library, University of Kansas).

Sir Barry Jackson, Collection towards a monograph on William Poel and his work in the theatre (manuscript dossier 1948, Royal Shakespeare Theatre Collection, Shakespeare Centre, Stratford-upon-Avon).

Paul Shelving designs held in Raymond Mander and Joe Mitchenson Theatre Collection.

Notes and References

INTRODUCTION

1. J. L. Styan, *The Shakespeare Revolution* (Cambridge, 1977).
2. Ibid., p. 6.
3. Cecil Chisholm, *Repertory: An Outline of the Modern Theatre Movement* (London, 1934) p. 54.
4. John Drinkwater, *Discovery* (London, 1932), p. 166.

CHAPTER ONE: THE FIRST NIGHT

1. All reviews of the first production of *Twelfth Night* are from a collection of undated press clippings (Birmingham Repertory Theatre Archive, Birmingham Central Library). The press book for 1913–1918 is missing.
2. Cecil Chisholm, *Repertory: An Outline of the Modern Theatre Movement* (London, 1934), p. 53.
3. Felix Aylmer, recalled in 'The Mighty Line', a radio broadcast devised by T. C. Kemp (19 November 1947).
4. John Drinkwater, *The Gentle Art of Theatre Going* (London, 1927), p. 24.
5. See Basil Dean, *Seven Ages* (London, 1970) and Ben Iden Payne, *A Life in a Wooden O* (New Haven, 1977).
6. Barry Jackson, 'Introduction' to Bache Matthews, *A History of the Birmingham Repertory Theatre* (London, 1924), p. xiv.
7. Herbert Beerbohm Tree quoted in Basil Dean, *Seven Ages*, p. 103.
8. A concise general survey of the repertory movement may be found in George Rowell and Anthony Jackson, *The Repertory Movement* (Cambridge, 1984).

9. Sir Barry Jackson, speech to Sheffield Playgoers' Society, 12 November 1913 (unpublished paper, Birmingham, 1913).
10. Ibid.
11. John Drinkwater, *Discovery* (London, 1932), pp. 154–155.
12. Sir Barry Jackson, speech to Sheffield Playgoers' Society.
13. P. P. Howe, *The Repertory Theatre: A Record and a Criticism* (London, 1910), p. 22.
14. Sir Barry Jackson, 'Literature and the Drama' (unpublished paper, Birmingham, 1920).

CHAPTER TWO:
SHAKESPEARE, BIRMINGHAM AND THE
PILGRIM PLAYERS

1. Stephen C. Schultz, 'Two Notes on William Poel's Sources' in *Nineteenth Century Theatre Research*, Vol. 2, no. 2 (autumn 1974), pp. 85–90.
2. Douglas A. Reid, 'Popular Theatre in Victorian Birmingham' in *Performance and Politics in Popular Drama*, ed. David Bradby, Louis James and Bernard Sharratt (Cambridge, 1980), pp. 65–89.
3. F. J. Furnivall, opening address for New Shakspere Society (30 March 1874) *New Shakspere Society Transactions* Vol. 1 (1874), p. x.
4. Minutes of the Birmingham Shakespeare Reading Society meetings, programmes and posters are held in Birmingham Central Library.
5. John Drinkwater, *Discovery*, p. 83.
6. John Drinkwater, *The Gentle Art of Theatre Going* (London, 1927), pp. 22–23.
7. Sir Barry Jackson, 'Producing the Comedies' in *Shakespeare Survey* Vol. 8 (1955), pp. 74–80.
8. Quoted in J. C. Trewin, *The Birmingham Repertory Theatre 1913–1963* (London, 1963), p. 4.
9. E. Harcourt Williams, *Four Years at the Old Vic* (London, 1935), p. 29.
10. Sir Barry Jackson, 'Producing the Comedies', pp. 75–6.
11. Max Beerbohm, 'Two Performances of Shakespeare, February 24, 1900', in *Around Theatres* (London, 1953), pp. 61–5.
12. Sir Barry Jackson, 'Producing the Comedies', p. 76.
13. Sir Sidney Lee, 'Mr Benson and Shakespearean Drama', in *Shakespeare and the Modern Stage* (London, 1906), p. 120.
14. John Drinkwater, *Discovery*, pp. 131–2.
15. Garry O'Connor, *Ralph Richardson: An Actor's Life* (London, 1982), pp. 30–1.

16. Edward Gordon Craig, quoted in Robert Speaight, *William Poel and the Elizabethan Revival* (London, 1954), pp. 165–6.
17. John Drinkwater, *Discovery*, p. 143.
18. Ibid., p. 149.
19. John Drinkwater, *Discovery*, p. 170.
20. Sir Barry Jackson, 'What We Did', (unpublished paper, Birmingham, 1921).
21. William Archer 'A Plea for an Endowed Theatre' in the *Fortnightly Review* Vol. 45, New Series (1 January–1 June 1889), pp. 610–626, p. 617.
22. Sir Barry Jackson, 'The Repertory Movement' (unpublished paper, Birmingham, 1932).

CHAPTER THREE: THE FIRST PILGRIM EXPERIMENTS

1. Sir Barry Jackson, letter to J. C. Trewin in 1959, quoted in *The Birmingham Repertory Theatre 1913–1963*, p. 4.
2. John Stokes, 'The Aesthetic Theatre: The Career of E. W. Godwin', in his *Resistible Theatres* (London, 1972), pp. 33–68.
3. Sir Barry Jackson, 'The Artist and the Theatre', speech to Birmingham Art Circle (unpublished paper, Birmingham, 1921).
4. John Stokes, 'A Wagner Theatre: Professor Herkomer's Pictorial-Musical Plays', in *Resistible Theatres*, pp. 71–110.
5. Sir Barry Jackson, 'Producing the Comedies', p. 77.
6. Edward Gordon Craig, 'Artistic Debauchery, An Extract from the writings of George Moore with a note by the Editor', *The Mask*, Vol. 4, no. 1 (July 1911), pp. 34–36, p. 35.
7. Edward Gordon Craig, *On the Art of the Theatre* (London, 1911; reissued London, 1957), p. 23.
8. Sir Barry Jackson, 'Literature and the Drama' (unpublished paper, Birmingham, 1920).
9. Bache Matthews, *A History of the Birmingham Repertory Theatre*, p. 7.
10. Carey Mazer, *Shakespeare Refashioned* (Ann Arbor, 1981), pp. 73–4.
11. F. Charlton Fry, *Charles Fry, his Life and Work* (London, 1932).
12. Maud Tree, quoted in *Herbert Beerbohm Tree: Some Memories of Him and his Art*, collected by Max Beerbohm (London, 1920), p. 124.
13. George Brandes, 'Introduction' to *The Two Gentlemen of Verona*, Favourite Classics (London, 1907), p. vi.
14. Robert Speaight, *William Poel and the Elizabethan Revival*, p. 120.
15. Sir Barry Jackson, 'Producing the Comedies', p. 77.
16. Robert Speaight, *William Poel and the Elizabethan Revival*, pp. 99–100.

17. Sir Barry Jackson, 'A Day at the Repertory Theatre', speech to Birmingham Repertory Playgoers's Society, 1 October 1922 (unpublished paper, Birmingham, 1922).

18. Sir Barry Jackson, Collection towards a monograph of William Poel and his work in the theatre (manuscript dossier, 1948). Held in Royal Shakespeare Theatre Collection, Shakespeare Centre, Stratford-upon-Avon.

19. Sir Barry Jackson, 'Review of Robert Speaight, *William Poel and the Elizabethan Revival*', *Shakespeare Quarterly*, Vol. VI (1955), pp. 89–90 (p. 90).

20. Sir Barry Jackson, letter to William Poel (28 August 1925). (Unpublished letter MS 32A, Kenneth Spencer Research Library, University of Kansas).

21. Carey Mazer, *Shakespeare Refashioned*, p. 65.

22. Diana Devlin, *A Speaking Part: Lewis Casson and the Theatre of his Time*, (London, 1982), p. 31.

23. Bache Matthews, *A History of the Birmingham Repertory Theatre*, p. 131.

24. Simon Williams, *Shakespeare on the German Stage* Vol. I: *1586–1914*, (Cambridge, 1990), pp. 185–215.

25. C. B. Purdom, *Granville Barker* (London, 1955), pp. 118–119.

26. Sam. N. Cooke, 'The Building' in Bache Matthews, *A History of the Birmingham Repertory Theatre*, p. 157.

27. Bamber Gascoigne, *Observer*, 3 November 1963.

CHAPTER FOUR: SHAKESPEARE IN THE NEW THEATRE

1. Rex Pogson, *Miss Horniman and the Gaiety Theatre, Manchester* (London, 1952), p. 159.

2. John Drinkwater, 'A Personal Note' in Bache Matthews, *A History of the Birmingham Repertory Theatre*, p. 176.

3. Ibid., p. 175.

4. John Drinkwater, *Discovery*, p. 167.

5. Gwen Ffrangçon-Davies in conversation with the author, May 1984.

6. John Gielgud, *An Actor and his Time* (London, 1979), p. 64.

7. Sally Beauman, *The Royal Shakespeare Company*, pp. 90–91.

8. Ibid., p. 90.

9. Tom English in conversation with the author, May 1983.

10. Alan Hughes, *Henry Irving, Shakespearean* (Cambridge, 1981), p. 227.

11. Sir Barry Jackson, 'Producing the Comedies', p. 75.

12. Maud Gill, *See the Players*, (London, 1938), p. 189.
13. Sir Barry Jackson, 'Producing the Comedies', p. 78.
14. Bache Matthews, *A History of the Birmingham Repertory Theatre*, facing p. 64 and p. 66.

CHAPTER FIVE:
NEW DIRECTORS, A NEW DESIGNER AND THE
FIRST LONDON PRODUCTION

1. Harley Granville-Barker, *The Exemplary Theatre* (London, 1922).
2. Ibid., p. 226.
3. Claude Lovat Fraser, 'The Art of the Theatre' in *The Studio*, Vol. 82 (November 1921), pp. 210–212; p. 212.
4. J. C. Trewin, *The Birmingham Repertory Theatre 1913–1963*, p. 59.
5. Finlay James in conversation with Tessa Sidey in her 'Paul Shelving —a Life in the Theatre', in *Paul Shelving (1888-1968) Stage Designer*, catalogued and edited by Tessa Sidey (Birmingham, 1986), p. 16.
6. Horace Shipp, 'The Artist in the Dressing Room' in *The Robes of Thespis*, edited for Rupert Mason by George Sheringham and R. Boyd Morrison (London, 1928), pp. 137–143, p. 141.
7. Paul Shelving, 'Stage Design' in *Theatre World* (January 1927), p. 22.
8. Bache Matthews, *A History of the Birmingham Repertory Theatre*, p. 136.
9. Ibid., p. 138.
10. Paul Shelving, *Birmingham Gazette* (14 February 1953).
11. J. C. Trewin, *Benson and the Bensonians* (London, 1960), p. 137.
12. Harcourt Williams, *Four Years at the Old Vic*, pp. 20–22, pp. 25–26.
13. Sally Beauman, *The Royal Shakespeare Company*, p. 91.
14. Bache Matthews, *A History of the Birmingham Repertory Theatre*, pp. 133–4.
15. J. C. Trewin, *The Birmingham Repertory Theatre 1913–1963*, p. 97.
16. Ibid., p. 130.
17. James Bridie, *One Way of Living* (London, 1939), p. 280.
18. Ralph Richardson, 'The Rep — forty years on' in *Birmingham Mail* (16 February 1953).
19. George Bernard Shaw, 'Juggins has worked the part out for himself uncommonly well. I have said so little to him that he is scared lest I should have given him up for hopeless', letter to Harley Granville Barker, 12 April 1911, in Eric Salmon, *Granville Barker and his Correspondents* (Detroit, 1986), p. 119.

20. Bache Matthews, *A History of the Birmingham Repertory Theatre*, p. 127.
21. Ralph Richardson, 'The Rep — forty years on'.
22. David Ayliff, 'Henry Kiell Ayliff and Paul Shelving', in *Paul Shelving (1888–1968) Stage Designer*, p. 25.
23. Garry O'Connor, *An Actor's Life*, p. 52.
24. John Gielgud, *Early Stages* (London, 1939), p. 70.
25. Bache Matthews, *A History of the Birmingham Repertory Theatre*, opposite p. 138; the curtain is also identified as a Street Scene for *The Two Gentlemen of Verona* in *The Studio*, Vol. 93 (1927) p. 263.
26. R. Crompton Rhodes, 'Shakespearean Methods at the Birmingham Repertory Theatre' in *The Stagery of Shakespeare* (Birmingham, 1922).
27. John Gielgud, *Early Stages*, p. 69.
28. Ibid., p. 69.
29. Gwen Ffrangçon-Davies, in conversation with the author, May 1984.
30. Ibid.

CHAPTER SIX:
THE FIRST MODERN-DRESS PRODUCTIONS

1. G. C. Lichtenberg, letter (October 1775), quoted by H. K. Ayliff, 'With Shakespeare to Savile Row' in *The Graphic*, 26 May 1928.
2. Robert Speaight, *Shakespeare on the Stage* (London, 1973), p. 202, p. 208.
3. H. K. Ayliff, 'With Shakespeare to Savile Row'.
4. Sir Barry Jackson, 'Producing the Comedies'.
5. Sir Barry Jackson, Review of *William Poel and the Elizabethan Revival* by Robert Speaight, *Shakespeare Quarterly*, Vol. 6 (1955) p. 89.
6. John Addington Symonds quoted by William Poel, *Shakespeare in the Theatre* (London, 1913; reissued, New York, 1968), p. 9.
7. Sir Barry Jackson, 'Literature and the Drama' (unpublished paper, October, 1920).
8. I am indebted to a detailed account of this production of *Cymbeline* in Janet Birkett, '*Cymbeline* in the Twentieth Century' (unpublished doctoral thesis, University of Birmingham, 1983).
9. H. K. Ayliff quoted in 'A Noted S. African producer', an interview syndicated in several South African newspapers including *Cape Argus*, 19 May 1928.
10. Bache Matthews, *History of the Birmingham Repertory Theatre*, pp. 101–2.

11. H. K. Ayliff, 'With Shakespeare to Savile Row'.
12. Cedric Hardwicke, *Let's Pretend* (London, 1932), p. 127.
13. H. K. Ayliff, 'With Shakespeare to Savile Row'.
14. Harley Granville Barker 'Introduction to *Cymbeline*', *The Player's Shakespeare*, Vol. II (London, 1923), p. xv.
15. Diana Devlin, *A Speaking Part*, pp. 139–40.
16. Harley Granville Barker, 'Introduction to *Macbeth*', *The Player's Shakespeare*, Vol. II (London, 1923) p. xxi.
17. Gordon Crosse, unpublished MS Diaries, Vol. IX (March 1925). (Shakespeare Library, Birmingham Central Library).
18. Barry Jackson, *The Birmingham Repertory Newsletter*, No. 5, edited by Alan Bland (August 1925).
19. According to the stage manager's notes, the curtain went up at 8.15pm and came down at 11.20pm with an interval of twelve minutes.
20. Cedric Hardwicke, *Let's Pretend*, p. 157.
21. *Tailor and Cutter*, quoted in *Birmingham Despatch*, 1 September 1925.
22. John Palmer, '*Hamlet* in Modern Dress' in *The Fortnightly Review* No. 707. New Series (2 November 1925), pp. 675–683.
23. Gordon Crosse, Diaries, Vol. IX, (September 1925).
24. Cedric Hardwicke, *Let's Pretend*, p. 158.
25. William Poel, unpublished letter (Barry Jackson Archive, Birmingham Central Library), 26 August 1925.
26. Peter Hall, '*Hamlet* Today' quoted by Stanley Wells, *Royal Shakespeare* (Manchester, 1977), p. 24.

CHAPTER SEVEN: MODERN-DRESS SHAKESPEARE

1. Joseph G. Price, *The Unfortunate Comedy* (Liverpool, 1968), p. 49. Price devotes four sentences to the production.
2. Robert Speaight, *William Poel and the Elizabethan Revival*, p. 233. However, a review of the production in *The Athenæum* (4 June 1920) refers only to 'The sombreness of the Elizabethan stage-setting'.
3. George Bernard Shaw, *Saturday Review* (2 February 1895), quoted in *Shaw on Shakespeare*, edited by Edwin Wilson (Harmondsworth, 1969), p. 34.
4. T. C. Kemp and J. C. Trewin, *The Stratford Festival* (Birmingham 1953), p. 128.
5. William Shakespeare, *All's Well that Ends Well*, edited by Arthur Quiller Couch and John Dover Wilson (London, 1929), Introduction, p. xi.

6. *Spring Cleaning* by Frederick Lonsdale was first performed in London in 1925. *Fallen Angels* by Noël Coward was staged in London in 1927.
7. H. K. Ayliff, 'With Shakespeare to Savile Row'.
8. For a photograph of the final scene see J. C. Trewin, *Birmingham Repertory Theatre 1913–1963*, opposite p. 49.
9. Sir Barry Jackson, *Evening News* (26 January 1928).
10. Joseph Price, *The Unfortunate Comedy*, opposite p. 54.
11. Sir Barry Jackson, *Evening News* (1 March 1927).
12. Tori Haring-Smith, *From Farce to Metadrama: A Stage History of 'The Taming of the Shrew' 1594–1983* (Westport, 1985), pp. 112–116. J. C. Trewin, *Birmingham Repertory Theatre 1913–1963*, p. 96: 'Ayliff had done it in New York where he was not invited to the opening because the Shubert management had lost heart; he had to stand at the back and listen to the cheering'.
13. The joke may also have derived from the comedy *Knock* by Jules Romain which was translated and staged by Harley Granville Barker at the Royalty Theatre in 1926 and produced at the Rep by W. G. Fay in March 1928.
14. Graham Holderness, *Shakespeare in Performance: 'The Taming of the Shrew'* (Manchester, 1989).
15. George Bishop, *Barry Jackson and the London Theatre* (London, 1933; reissued New York, 1969), p. 91.
16. Norman Marshall, *The Producer and the Play*, (London, 1957), pp. 175–176.
17. J. L. Styan, *The Shakespeare Revolution*, p. 150.
18. George Bishop, *Barry Jackson and the London Theatre*, p. 81.
19. Gordon Crosse, Diaries, Vol. XI (February 1928).
20. *Journey's End* was given its first performance by the Incorporated Stage Society at the Apollo Theatre on 9 December 1929. Laurence Olivier played Captain Stanhope.
21. T. C. Kemp, *The Birmingham Repertory Theatre* (Birmingham, 1943; second edition revised, 1948), p. 23.
22. Harley Granville Barker, Introduction to *Prefaces to Shakespeare, First Series* (London, 1927), p. xxxii.
23. T. C. Kemp, *The Birmingham Repertory Theatre*, p. 5.

NOTES TO THE EPILOGUE

1. Sir Barry Jackson, 'On Producing *Henry VI*' in *Shakespeare Survey, Vol. 6* (1953), pp. 49–52; p. 49.

2. Michael Gambon quoted in Peter Lewis, *The National: A Dream Made Concrete* (London, 1990), p. 29.
3. Michael Billington, 'Is There a Crisis in Shakespearean Acting?', *Guardian* (10 April 1987).

Index

171

176